THE GIRL IN BUILDING C

July 1942

"JANE"

THE GIRL IN BUILDING C

The True Story of a Teenage Tuberculosis Patient

EDITED BY

Mary Krugerud

MINNESOTA
HISTORICAL
SOCIETY PRESS

CLEAN
WATER
LAND &
LEGACY
AMENDMENT

www.mnhspress.org

The Minnesota Historical Society Press is a member of the Association of University Presses.

Manufactured in the United States of America

10 9 8 7 6 5 4 3 2 1

♾ The paper used in this publication meets the minimum requirements of the American National Standard for Information Sciences—Permanence for Printed Library Materials, ANSI Z39.48-1984.

International Standard Book Number
ISBN: 978-1-68134-095-1 (paper)
ISBN: 978-1-68134-096-8 (e-book)

Library of Congress Cataloging-in-Publication Data
Names: Barnes, Marilyn J., 1927– author. | Krugerud, Mary, editor. | Minnesota
    Historical Society Press, publisher.
Title: The girl in building C : the true story of a teenage tuberculosis patient /
    edited by Mary Krugerud.
Other titles: True story of a teenage tuberculosis patient
Description: St. Paul, MN : The Minnesota Historical Society Press, [2018] |
    Includes bibliographical references and index.
Identifiers: LCCN 2018022614 | ISBN 9781681340951 (pbk. : alk. paper) | ISBN
    9781681340968 (ebook)
Subjects: | MESH: Barnes, Marilyn J., 1927– | Minnesota Sanatorium for Consump-
    tives. | Tuberculosis, Pulmonary—rehabilitation | Hospitalization | Adolescent
    | Inpatients | Minnesota | Collected Correspondence
Classification: LCC RC310 | NLM WF 330 | DDC 616.99/500835—dc23
LC record available at https://lccn.loc.gov/2018022614

This and other Minnesota Historical Society Press books are available from popular e-book vendors.

This book is dedicated to Marilyn Barnes Robertz
and the more than fifty thousand people who sought
to be healed at one of Minnesota's state, county,
or private tuberculosis sanatoriums

THE GIRL IN BUILDING C

THE GIRL IN BUILDING C

INTRODUCTION

SOMETIMES, WHEN ALL YOU ARE DOING IS LOOKING FOR INFORMA-
tion, a gift appears. In 2015, I received a Legacy Research Fellowship
award from the Minnesota Historical Society to study the history of
tuberculosis treatment at Minnesota's sanatoriums. One of the subjects, Ah-gwah-ching State Sanatorium at Walker, is well documented
in the society's government collection, but I was hoping to find
something more personal—a diary, perhaps. Instead, I found the
Marilyn J. Barnes papers. Not just a haphazard collection of papers,
but more than three hundred articulate letters written from a young
Ah-gwah-ching patient to her parents during World War II. I hoped
to connect with someone who remembered this delightful person
and could tell me more about her. Instead, I found Marilyn, very alive
and alert at age eighty-eight. We talked on the telephone, and then
we met. I knew her experience deserved to be more than a footnote
to Ah-gwah-ching's history, and so began a series of interviews that
grew into a book and produced a friendship. *The Girl in Building C* is
her story.

* * *

Marilyn Barnes, age sixteen, lived in St. Peter, Minnesota, with her
parents, Virginia and Wayland, known locally as Bill. A high school
student with good grades, she was active in band and chorus at school
and church. While attending an event in Minneapolis, she shared a
hotel room with a girl from another town. The girl coughed a lot, and
Marilyn later developed a cold with a cough that did not go away but
became progressively worse. Marilyn had a fever and lost weight. She
coughed up blood, alarming her parents, who brought her to the doc-

tor. He admitted her to the hospital in St. Peter, where a skin test and an x-ray confirmed that she had tuberculosis.

Between 1912 and 1918, thirty-five of Minnesota's eighty-seven counties responded to legislation authorizing the construction and maintenance of tuberculosis sanatoriums within a district system. Because Nicollet County did not belong to one of the fourteen existing districts, Marilyn was transported to Ah-gwah-ching State Sanatorium near Walker. Ah-gwah-ching's forested campus overlooked the shores of Leech Lake, 225 miles from Marilyn's home and family in St. Peter. The ambulance she rode in did double duty as the hearse for a funeral home because St. Peter did not have a formal ambulance service at the time. Her parents traveled with her to the sanatorium, where she was admitted on October 28, 1943. She would stay for almost three years.

For the duration of her treatment, she wrote frequently to her family. Her mother saved the 303 precious cards and letters that linked her and Marilyn during this span. Marilyn Barnes Robertz donated her letters and photographs to the Minnesota Historical Society in 2010. As letters written from a tuberculosis sanatorium, they contain stories about uplifting life experiences and sobering encounters with death. As letters written during World War II, they are home-front missives describing how the patients were touched by events and consequences of the war.

The Disease

Tuberculosis, an infectious disease caused by Mycobacterium tuberculosis, generally affects the lungs and is called pulmonary TB; when it occurs elsewhere in the body it is called extra-pulmonary. The bacteria is spread by coughing, sneezing, and spitting. A person can be infected but not have active TB and then is not contagious. Active disease, if not treated, kills about half of infected people. Historically, TB was called consumption because of the symptoms of weight loss and wasting away.

The **Letters**

Excerpts from the letters and postcards were chosen to illustrate the daily life of a sanatorium as seen from a hospital bed. The writer is a teenager, and the correspondence displays the innocence and perspective of a young girl. Some remarks reflecting the era's culture may be regarded as offensive today; those comments have not been deleted or edited but have been given context. References to people who were not directly involved in Marilyn's hospitalization or recovery have been omitted. Day and date headings are included, with information added in brackets if not given on the original correspondence. Salutations—which were usually a variation on "Dear Folks" or "Dear Mom, Daddy, Grams, and Keith"—have been included only if the letter was addressed to other people. Marilyn signed most of her correspondence with "Lots of Love, Marilyn." Only unusual closings have been included. Marilyn often used a plus sign ("+") instead of the word "and." An ampersand ("&") has been substituted in the text. Where she spelled names phonetically, the correct spelling is in brackets.

Sources

Explanatory material was gathered from:

Ah-gwah-ching's archival records at the Minnesota Historical Society's Gale Family Library,

Invited and Conquered: Historical Sketch of Tuberculosis in Minnesota by J. Arthur Myers,

A Brief History of the Minnesota State Sanatorium by Skip Oliver,

articles in the *St. Peter Herald*, and

interviews with Marilyn conducted by the author in 2017.

Exceptions appear in the end notes.

1. ARRIVAL, OCTOBER 1943

Tell all my friends to write

STATE SANATORIUM, AH-GWAH-CHING, MINNESOTA, CII

OCT. 29, 1943

Well, today I'm feeling just swell. Just had dinner and boy, you should have seen what I ate. Was real hungry, too. Of all things—guess what??! Actual live, <u>honest to goodness bananas</u> with lemon pie. Yum! Yum!

■ The first paragraph of Marilyn's first letter home mentioned food, not homesickness or her health. Fresh bananas and lemons were a rare commodity in most homes because, after nearly three years of war on the European and Pacific fronts, rationing of supplies in the United States was taking its toll. The sanatorium, though operating under a similar system, received a larger allotment of fresh fruit and vegetables because of its status as a hospital. Marilyn loved pie, and her mother rarely made it. She was happy to learn it was on the menu for dessert every Friday.

* * *

The weather is just gorgeous up here and Mabel and I have the swellest view from our window. Right now the upper window is open about 2½ feet, and the fresh air is pouring in.

■ New patients at Ah-gwah-ching were commonly assigned to rooms with two or three beds. Marilyn's only roommate, Mabel Bakalar, was not too much older than she. Marilyn noted in her letter that *Mabel and I are good pals, and she is nicer today than she seemed at first.* Because absolute bed rest was a mandatory requirement for new arrivals, compatibility with a roommate was essential. There were no privacy curtains and few distractions besides reading or writing. The fresh, pine-scented air was no longer considered as integral to the tuberculosis cure as it had been at the turn of the century, but it remained part of a germ-fighting arsenal. In the absence of a forced-air heating or cooling system, the open windows circulated outdoor air throughout the building. This benefitted not only the patients but also the staff, who were exposed to bacteria expelled via coughs and sneezes.

* * *

Had a bath this morning and am spitting up stuff for specimens.

Testing phlegm or sputum was the surest way of determining whether someone had tuberculosis. Marilyn's "stuff" would be injected into a guinea pig. In six weeks, the guinea pig would be autopsied. If tubercles were present in the animal, the diagnosis would be active tuberculosis. When very ill, patients produced a lot of sputum. They were told to expectorate rather than swallow their sputum because the tubercle bacillus can survive stomach acid and enter the intestines. From there, TB can spread via the lymph system to other organs in the body. Patients had to cover their mouths when they coughed or sneezed and collect their sputum in a container, never in a handkerchief. Bed patients had metal cups with a disposable liner. Mobile patients carried a small waxed cardboard cup. Cups and liners were collected daily by nurse's aides and incinerated.

In the sanatorium, certain things were considered clean and others were contaminated. The patients were contaminated. Marilyn hated that word, used over and over by doctors and nurses. "People were afraid of us," she said, "and to have people afraid of me was a real shock."

* * *

Then they took blood out of my arm for blood test and count and gave me another Mantoux test. Will know how it turns out in a few days or maybe even tomorrow.

■ The Mantoux test consists of injecting a small amount of TB antigens under the skin, usually in the forearm. A reddened swelling at Marilyn's injection site gave evidence of exposure to tuberculosis but did not necessarily signify an active case. A follow-up x-ray revealed dark areas of her lung that suggested a tuberculous cavity.

* * *

The doctor is a lady, Dr. Gorenflo, and she came into our room this morning. Will be having an examination from her either this afternoon or tomorrow.

Johnson & Johnson sputum cup and holder

Building C at Ah-gwah-ching

■ At Ah-gwah-ching, physicians were assigned by building. Marilyn's "C" building had opened in 1932 and consisted of four floors. The lower floors contained the treatment rooms, operating rooms, and medical offices. The morgue was a half story below, just off the tunnel that connected buildings. The second and third floors had thirteen patients' rooms each, all facing south and having a double window apiece. Marilyn's room was on the second floor, in the middle of the building. The north side contained a few patients' rooms, nurses' offices, linen closets, bathrooms, and utility rooms. The fourth floor had two large wards at either end with seven patient rooms in the middle. A fourth-floor terrace wrapped around three sides of the building and was used for sun treatments known as heliotherapy. The attic had storage rooms. The second floor of the C building housed women, and Marilyn's assigned doctor was Leila Gorenflo, one of several female doctors who worked at sanatoriums in Minnesota. Marilyn did get her exam that day, but not from Gorenflo. A male doctor told her that the trouble was in her left lung, but he wouldn't give details because he wasn't "her" doctor. All new patients suffered through the wait for a formal diagnosis.

* * *

Say, is all this care payed for by the state? That's what Mabel said. Answer please.

■ Payment for a sanatorium stay depended on several factors. Patients were eligible for entrance to Ah-gwah-ching if they had been residents of the state for one year. When Marilyn arrived, the charge for care was $2.28 a day. Patients or their families paid all or a portion of the fee if possible. Although the state subsidized the institution, there were no "free" beds. For patients unable to pay anything, the state would pay five dollars a week and their home county was charged for the balance. This policy aligned with that of the district sanatoriums, which were supported by a combination of county tax levies, state aid, and patient payments. Marilyn's father worked as a mail carrier for the US post office in St. Peter. He paid the whole cost at first. Later in her stay, he asked the county commissioners for assistance, and they reduced the price he had to pay.

* * *

Now for some of the things I'd like you to send me. 1st – Pajamas (3 pr). You won't have to send them all at once. 2nd – Don't send the Star Journal as Mabel gets it, but I'd love to get The Herald and, of course, the School Paper. 3rd – Write real, real often as I'm terribly homesick. Tell all my friends to write. Remember to write Ah-gwah-ching, Minn. and C.II! Bye now.

■ Marilyn's trip by ambulance to the sanatorium had been rushed, with little time for planning or packing. She asked her parents to send her clothing because patients did not wear hospital gowns. Those confined to bed wore pajamas. Newspapers and letters maintained the ties to home. Patients were not allowed to use the floor's only telephone, which was in the nurses' office.

Marilyn's requested items arrived in a box her parents sent via the Greyhound bus, which was less expensive than mailing a package. They could put a package on a bus in the morning, and it would arrive in Walker on the last bus of the day and be delivered to the sanatorium. Sometimes her family shipped things by walking to the train depot and handing a package directly to the mail-car employee, not even going to the post office first.

Marilyn specified Ah-gwah-ching as the sanatorium's address because the absence of the word "sanatorium" was important. Tuberculosis was still a dreaded disease that carried a stigma, and patients didn't want the words "sanatorium" or "tuberculosis" to be on the envelope. While Marilyn's family chose to be frank about her whereabouts, others invented stories about long trips and visits to distant relatives to conceal the actual location of their family members.

OCTOBER 30, 1943, 3 P.M.
Right now we are listening to the Minn. football game. (I got a new pair of plastic ear-phones.)

■ Marilyn recorded the time on her return address because she was hoping to include this letter in the outgoing afternoon mail. The mail train made two runs a day through Walker; Ah-gwah-ching had outgoing mail bags picked up on-the-fly on a catcher hook near the sanatorium at 9:30 AM and 4 PM. Incoming mail arrived the same way and was distributed at 10 AM and 4:50 PM. Because mail was sorted and bagged in the postal car on the train, the turnaround time was swift. Many of Marilyn's letters were written three days apart, with her parents' responses arriving between hers.

Patients were not allowed to have personal radios. Like many other sanatoriums, Ah-gwah-ching was wired for radio, with the base unit in the main office. Each bed had an earphone plug-in next to it, so patients could listen individually and keep noise to a minimum. Because only one radio station could be broadcast at a time, patients listened to whatever the switchboard operator chose, which was often WCCO radio, 830 AM in Minneapolis. The patients stayed current with war news and enjoyed musical broadcasts, sports, and radio comedies and dramas. For a short time, a patients' radio program called station AHEM was run by Joe Ring with records furnished by Melvin Miner. When Joe was discharged in April 1944, it went off the air.

* * *

Haven't done much today but rest and take my pulse and temp. They do that every 2 hrs for the 1st 4 days you are here. Gosh but it gets tiresome!

■ Another tiresome part of the daily routine was a morning dose of laxative to keep digestive systems regular and promote bowel movements. "Awful," said Marilyn.

* * *

None of the doctors seem to come and take care of me and so I don't have the least idea how good or bad I'm off. My Mantoux test is red (positive) but no one has come to look at it. This is getting to sound like I'm an awful complainer but the meals are really nothing to write home about.

■ Dr. J. A. Myers, professor of medicine at the University of Minnesota, said, "Nothing results in more dissatisfaction among patients than insufficient, poorly prepared or improperly served food. . . . Patients themselves have known best the great importance of cooks in sanatoriums. It is the cooks who have made the food palatable and thus have kept many patients in sanatoriums who otherwise would have left against advice."[1] Cooks responsible for preparing tempting food for three hundred patients plus employees were especially challenged during the war, when supplies of sugar, coffee, tea, cocoa, ketchup, and spices were limited. In addition, more than half the patients couldn't go to the dining room, and their food needed to arrive hot at bedside. Sanatorium food was generally better in the summer, with fresh fruits and vegetables from the huge garden. Meat was served at least once every day because the sanatorium farm staff raised cows, pigs, turkeys, and chickens and did their own slaughtering. The importance of food is evident in Marilyn's letters. Almost all include a summary of her meals.

* * *

Oh mommy and daddy, I get so homesick to see you that I hardly can hold back the tears. Every nite I just about cry myself to sleep! It's okay up here but how I just long to be at Glen Lake. I wouldn't be so far away from home then.

■ Marilyn's uncle Gerold and aunt Ruth Laumann lived in Minneapolis, and Hennepin County's Glen Lake Sanatorium was about fifteen miles away from them and on a bus line. They suggested that Marilyn transfer to Glen Lake to be closer to them. Excerpts from Ruth's October 26 and November 2 letters to Marilyn's mother, Virginia, show concern for their niece.

> The reason that we called you back last night to suggest Glen Lake was that we know so much about the place and feel she would be so much happier there, than so far away. . . . Our thot was we and others close to her could get out to cheer her for a few minutes when permitted, and then the thing is that you folks could see her often enough to personally check on her. And believe it or not that's something I'd want to do if it was my girl. Remember that Walker is a long ways from St. Peter. We aren't trying to tell you what to do with her, but we are very fond of Marilyn also and feel so vitally interested in her welfare.

Virginia's cousin Dorothy Koch chimed in with the same push for Glen Lake in an October 27 letter: "If it were Dorothea instead of Marilyn, I would not send her to Walker—the main reason being that it is too far away from home for you to keep in touch with her progress. Then, too, Walker is no better than Glen Lake, in fact I would prefer Glen Lake."

Glen Lake was probably not an option for Marilyn. Because her home was not in Hennepin County, her family would have been charged the higher nonresident rate. If her father couldn't pay the full amount, Nicollet County would not have been obligated to help financially. Glen Lake usually accepted nonresidents on a short-term basis only, for special care or surgery not available at their home institution. All sanatoriums were experiencing nursing shortages because of World War II. Glen Lake had decreased its bed capacity and might not have had room anyway.

* * *

Please, Please come up soon. I can hardly stand it not seeing you. If you haven't much gas, why don't you take the bus?

▧ The war affected travel, and mandatory gas rationing had begun on December 1, 1942. Gas was not in short supply, but rubber for tires was. Limiting gas was the easiest way to curb unnecessary travel. Marilyn's parents could ride a Greyhound bus from St. Peter to Minneapolis and transfer to another that would let them off within walking distance of Ah-gwah-ching.

* * *

Got a swell pile of letters in the mail this morn. Was real glad to get The Herald and will probably get the school paper Mon. Now comes another dreary part! Goodness but I'm sure writing an awful un-cheery letter! These are some of the things I need badly. 1) $3 or $5. I've had to buy quite a few things like stamps, cards, maybe a chest of drawers, etc. 2) My nail polish remover. It's probably in some drawer or shelf in bathroom. 3) New comb (preferably rat-tail). 4) Soap dish with a top cover. 5) Just found out I need slacks for when I go for a treatment. My green one will do but I sure wish I had some new flannel ones. This is quite a list of junk to send and if you'd send it all in a nice big box, I'd have it to put more stuff in. Am quite cramped as it is now.

P.S. Truthfully I'm really not enjoying myself here.

▧ Storage at the sanatorium was inadequate. Marilyn and Mabel were in a large room with two beds. Each had a bedside table with no drawers. There was a metal locker, divided in half, that could hold a few clothes. Some patients purchased miniature chests of drawers made by patients in an occupational therapy workshop

Marilyn's bedside cabinet, painted institutional green

using scrap wood from peach crates and other projects. Those cabinets were made to fit on top of the bedside table and had three drawers that could hold stationery, needlework, or books. Marilyn bought one, painted the same institutional green as the walls. Marilyn also provided her own soap—usually Lux or Camay—which lathered well in the sanatorium's hard water.

2. ADJUSTMENT

Anxious as ever to get out of this place

SUNDAY, OCT. 31ST, 1943

I guess you really don't know how much I love you and miss you. Life has certainly been miserable these past 3 days for me being stuck away up here away from all my loved ones. Might as well be 300,000 miles away as 300. Oh mommy, why oh why did I ever have to get such a thing? Guess I'm not such a grown-up person after all. Just a very homesick little girl aching for her family's affection and love. Everybody always said I was so brave about it but I'm certainly far from that. If I only could be home today listening to the symphony after doing the Sunday dinner dishes and Gran and Nita sitting there talking to Pegg and Mory. It's been awfully dreary up here, half raining and snowing with the sun never peeking out to say a cheery hello.

■ In addition to her mother and father, Marilyn missed her younger brother, Keith, and the family dog, Tippy. Also, she was close to her grandmother Alma Laumann and aunt Wilma Anita Laumann (known as Nita), who lived next door in a brick Queen Anne–style house built by Marilyn's great-grandparents in 1887. Aunt Peggy and Uncle Maurice (Mory) Laumann were also frequent visitors to her family home.

* * *

Mabel is sleeping now so didn't have anything to do. She helps a lot in keeping my mind off homesickness. We are swell pals, and we know another girl in a ward which we write to. Mabel's sister is so very sweet and her pals and she come to see us evenings, too, so that also helps pass time. Will see Gorenflo tomorrow morning so will find out all the dope. Everybody does some handiwork around here because the time passes so slow so thot I'd knit a sweater. There is a lady here I could have help me. She's just wonderful on handwork. Will be a little while before I can start but you could probably get me some yarn. Don't feel like writing anybody except you and my pals, so would appreciate it if you would let all the relatives know about me.

▓ Mabel's sister, Elsie, also had tuberculosis and was at Ah-gwah-ching. Her health improved, so she was on an open ward in Building B. A move to the B building was a form of graduation, as patients were often placed according to their stage of recovery. This sorting was typical of larger sanatoriums. Wards typically held up to fourteen patients with no privacy curtains.

* * *

Men's ward at Ah-Gwah-Ching

P.S. Have you had Mantoux test yet? Please tell me all about it.

▓ Because Marilyn had tuberculosis, all members of her family with whom she had close contact were required to have a tuberculin test. All tested negative, strengthening Marilyn's belief that she contracted tuberculosis from the girl at the church convention.

WEDNESDAY MORNING, 1943 [NOVEMBER 3]
I've been feeling pretty good and am eating bigger meals every day but don't expect to gain much the first month as all the energy goes to the T.B. I now weigh 103½.

▓ Marilyn's normal weight was around 125 and, at five-foot-six, she was naturally slender. Tuberculosis had an ancient name, consumption, that described a progressive wasting away. The disease can manifest in a long, slow decline accompanied by a fever that spikes and ebbs. In the lungs, it creates cavities and causes breathlessness and hemorrhages. If it spreads to other parts of the body, in the bones it literally gnaws at the structure and within internal organs it causes inflammation and sores.

* * *

Have you been asked for your consent for me taking pneumo?

▓ Artificial pneumothorax was one of several treatments for tuberculosis that appeared during the last decade of the nineteenth century. The procedure introduced air into the pleural cavity that exists between the two thin membranes that surround the lungs. As the lungs expand and contract, the membranes slide against each other with lubrication provided by a small amount of fluid. Inserting air into the gap between the membranes forces the lung to collapse. If a patient's lung had tuberculous lesions, this state of inactivity could prevent them from developing into cavities. If cavities had already developed, a collapsed lung would help the body create the fibroids needed to wall off and contain the germs within the cavity and also possibly prevent the bacteria from migrating into the sputum. Marilyn's doctor decided the procedure could be effective in her situation. Because she was a minor, her parents needed to give permission before she could "get air" or pneumo, as patients commonly called it.

* * *

Boy, does news travel fast here. By the 2nd day I was here, practically 3 whole wards knew Mabel had a new roommate her same age. Elsie and Margie Smith (her pal) come over every night and we have so much fun talking. That's the only time we can have kids visit us because we rest most of the other times.

▧ Sanatoriums assumed the characteristics of small towns, gossip included. A popular rhyme of that era claimed "A telegram is known for speed; a radiogram is sooner; but nothing yet can go as fast, as a sanatorium rumor."

FRIDAY THE 5TH, 6:30 A.M. [NOVEMBER]
Yesterday we had a beautiful snow all day and it made "our scene" out of the window so pretty. It was dark here that first nite, so you didn't get to see our south side surroundings. It's not actually a pine forest but more on the order of a park with brightly painted chairs here and there, trees and lawn and a winding sidewalk with a quaint little lamppost to light the way at night.

▧ Because Marilyn arrived in the evening, her knowledge of the sanatorium campus was limited to the view from her window. Ahgwah-ching, like many US sanatoriums, was built in a rural, wooded area. Dr. Edward Trudeau, who established the first well-known sanatorium in the United States, had recovered from tuberculosis at Saranac Lake in the 1880s. This convalescence in upstate New York's Adirondack Mountains led him to promote the fresh-air rest cure that became the norm. In 1901, Minnesota governor Samuel Van Sant appointed a sanatorium commission with authority to select a site for a state facility. The commission members recommended that a sanatorium be built near Walker, by Leech Lake in

Cass County. The desired seven hundred acres covered a small hill to the west of the lake, near an Ojibwe Indian reservation. Much of the forest had already been logged and was being reseeded. An open area large enough for a dairy herd, orchard, and vegetable garden could provide fresh comestibles for the patients. The sanatorium opened in December 1907 as the Minnesota State Sanatorium for Consumptives, with several open-air cottages for patients. The name officially changed in 1922, and, as more substantial brick buildings were constructed, the cottages were used as staff housing.

The alphabet buildings—A, B, C, and D—were connected by tunnels and/or walkways. E, also known as the Eagle Building, stood detached. Lakeside Building was the nurses' home. The Hall Memorial Pavilion, recreation hall, and administration buildings were multipurpose, with offices, treatment rooms, and dining halls. Various outbuildings included the superintendent's house, staff home, greenhouse, weather station gazebo, power plant, and engineer's cottage. There were two farm sites—one for animals and the other for crops.

* * *

Oh, folks, I wish you could have seen the sunrise this morning. The horizon is all purplish pink and yellow and tints the white fluffy clouds pink in the blue sky. This is all set off by the tall pines and touches of white on the ground. Never saw anything like it in St. Peter.

■ Marilyn appreciated her view of sunrises at Ah-gwah-ching. Her hometown of St. Peter is situated in the Minnesota River valley, and her family's house was near the river, not up on the bluffs. The orientation of her bedroom window there did not permit her to see the colorful display that is unique to the morning sun.

* * *

Every morning when the janitor comes in to bring our mail he always says, "You get all the mail around here!" And boy, I sure must have a monopoly on it, too.

■ Marilyn had been at Ah-gwah-ching less than two weeks, but she had received eight letters the previous morning and another one on the afternoon delivery. One contained an Irish linen handkerchief. Many people sent handkerchiefs as gifts, but the patients weren't allowed to use them. Anything used to collect body fluids was considered contaminated and had to be destroyed. Hankies could not be part of the laundry. Marilyn's pen pal, Nancy Stutz, sent the November issue of the *Ladies' Home Journal*, in which she had made little footnotes and remarks. Marilyn described it as "a whole letter strung out." The girls joined the pen pal club of *Child Life* magazine in eighth grade. Nancy, who lived in Ohio, continued writing to Marilyn throughout her sanatorium stay. Although they eventually lost touch, they reconnected much later in life. They were still corresponding in 2017 at age ninety.

* * *

I still cough quite a little but it's best to get it all out. Lately Mabel and I have been sleeping and resting a lot – never get out of bed.

■ Marilyn's letter was upbeat, but her ready acceptance of the total bed rest regimen indicated the severity of her illness.

MONDAY 8TH BEFORE BREAKFAST [NOVEMBER]
Have a few things to write again so here goes "while the going's good." We had a terrible blizzard here yesterday and it makes the whole landscape pretty. When the wind blows up here it groans like one of those big transit trucks, but I'm very used to it now. Yesterday we had just a swell dinner. Fried chicken (just delicious), mashed potatoes & gravy and dressing. Green beans, bread & butter, cranberry sauce, milk, and ice cream. Mabel and I ate until we almost had tummy aches.

■ Milk was an important part of daily menus, and Marilyn drank half-and-half between meals to get enough calories and fat in her diet. The transmission of bovine tuberculosis from cattle to humans via dairy products had been confirmed in 1904, so the sanatorium built a dairy barn in 1912 and established its own herd of registered Holstein cows to have a healthful, reliable source of milk and butter for patients.

* * *

We have a pet squirrel that climbs up the brick wall every day and sits up on his hind feet on our outside window sill. So cute as he cocks his head and looks in to see if we'll give him anything to eat.

▓ Patients' lives were so pared down to the basics that even a friendly squirrel was major entertainment. Marilyn and Mabel took joy where they found it. By opening the screen a bit, they could put out little nibbles of food for the squirrel.

* * *

Fixed my fingernails and put up my hair but still am takin' it very easy. . . . Mom, you said that you don't come up here for looks, but boy oh boy, after you get to feel a little better, you primp and primp just like everyone else does. Almost everyone has their hair and nails just done immaculately, and not by a beauty operator either.

▓ With so much time on their hands and only their upper bodies visible in bed, female patients paid a lot of attention to their hair and nails. Visitors were known to comment that the patients looked better than they themselves did. Patients could also be particular about their bathrobes and pajamas. Satin and quilted bed jackets, decorative and warm, were especially appreciated. Marilyn hinted for a chenille bathrobe as a Christmas gift.

* * *

Nita, wonder if you'd write just a little post card to Eileen and tell her I won't be writing for a while because of pneumo. Pneumo isn't really terrible as I make it sound because there is no pain or anything, just feel a little stiff the first couple of times and I'm not going to overdo myself.

▓ Marilyn's parents gave permission for pneumotherapy treatments. The doctor injected Novocain, inserted a hollow needle between Marilyn's ribs, and then introduced about 150 to 300 cubic centimeters of air until her lung achieved the desired state of collapse. The doctor worked gradually because it was unnerving to lose breathing capacity too quickly. The air would be slowly absorbed, so the procedure was repeated about every two weeks to maintain the collapse until healing was achieved.

* * *

You know what?? A <u>real</u> Indian nurse just came in to give us water. There are quite a few on the cure here, only they are in the Indian building, quite a ways from CII.

■ The presence of Native Americans was new to Marilyn, and she was kind of fascinated. The average tuberculosis mortality rate among Minnesota's Native population in the early 1900s was much higher—three to six times—than that of the state as a whole. In 1923, Ojibwe public health nurses had begun work on the Leech Lake and White Earth Indian reservations. Along with their other tasks, they disseminated information about tuberculosis and how it spreads. The nurses also encouraged infected people to submit to medical care. A group of concerned doctors and state officials persuaded Congress to remodel an Indian boarding school at Onigum on Leech Lake and use it as a sanatorium. Its eighty-five beds were soon full. It lacked x-ray equipment, a laundry, or a full-time physician. Although the two sanatoriums were across Shingobee Bay from each other and less than two miles apart via water, the trip by road was about eleven miles. To provide better care, plans were made in 1934 to construct a modern sanatorium building specifically for Native Americans at Ah-gwah-ching. The state deeded the land under the building to the federal government so the Bureau of Indian Affairs could finance the construction. The segregation of Native patients at Ah-gwah-ching was financial, based on the flow of federal funding for their cost of care and the maintenance of Building E.

SUNDAY MORNING, 9 A.M. [NOVEMBER 14]

Yesterday was visiting day for the patients. Guess what? We had 3 old gentlemen come in and see us. One man sells fancywork he does himself, and the second one just came in to talk (quite a funny old character, made us laugh a lot), and the 3rd old man was from St. Peter. A Mr. Schnyder or Schnieder, don't know how you spell it. Grandma would probably know him. He said he was a good friend of Judge Laumann, and I told him that he was my grandfather. He seemed so nice, and we knew a lot of the same people. He lives at the Hall Pavilion for men. They are mostly old gentlemen who can take care of themselves but will probably live here the rest of their life.

■ The third gentleman's name was Nels Snyder, and he continued to visit Marilyn every Saturday for a long time. They could share stories of "home." The Hall Pavilion memorialized Dr. P. M. Hall, the sanatorium's medical director from 1918 until he passed away in 1928. The building originally housed tuberculous children, but by the time of Marilyn's residency it was used for ambulatory patients and offices.

Although the Social Security Act of 1935 and the Old Age Assistance program provided some financial protection for the elderly, there were few housing options for those without family resources. Though appearing to be healed, some

**Marilyn and her friend
Nels Snyder from St. Peter**

patients continued to have positive sputum, excluding them from housing in poor farms and boardinghouses, which did not accept tenants with infectious diseases. Marilyn's gentlemen visitors may have been in that situation, and they were relatively free to roam the sanatorium grounds.

* * *

Time seems to go so much faster nowadays and I'm really what you might say – contented, although of course I'm still as anxious as ever to get out of this place.

■ Marilyn had been told that her stay might be two months. When she learned how long other people had been at Ah-gwah-ching, she realized it was going to be a while. Historians, sociologists, and physicians have written articles and books about the psychological, nonmedical aspects of patient behavior. Some reported that patients experienced a feeling of relative well-being even though they were dying. Some concluded that the so-called optimism of tuberculous patients was compensation for depression and suicidal trends. Compliance with a sanatorium's strict rules was seen by others to be evidence of intimidation by physicians. Marilyn appreciated the rigid routine of each day and believed it helped make the time go faster.

* * *

Just wanted to tell you something important now, Mom, that I forgot in your last letter. When you get some pajamas get a _real_ large size because they go through the laundry where they are boiled and they shrink and lose colors something terrible. Dr. Callahan dropped in especially to see me (I think) and he said that Dr. Gorenflo was very pleased with the way pneumo is working on me. I hope it's true.

■ Dr. Francis F. Callahan, age fifty-two, assumed the superintendent duties at Ah-gwah-ching in 1942. His predecessor, Dr. Herbert Burns, served in that capacity for fourteen years before taking a position with the State Board of Health. Dr. Callahan worked with the British army medical corps during World War I and, when he returned to Minnesota, became the medical director at the privately owned Pokegama Sanatorium near Pine City. It closed due to war shortages.

* * *

I sorta am hoping you'll come on Sunday and stay over Monday so you could see Dr. Gorenflo in the morning as she doesn't come on Sunday.

■ Marilyn's parents visited on Sunday, November 21.

3. HOLIDAYS 1943

Didn't seem like Christmas without you folks

FRIDAY MORNING, 7:00 A.M. [NOVEMBER 26]
Well, how'd you like to hear about our Thanksgiving feast up here? We had – or rather I had – the leg and 3 huge slices of white meat of turkey, Mashed Potatoes & Gravy, Sage Dressing, Cranberry sauce, Sliced raw tomato, Celery, Green olive and a ripe olive, bread & butter, Milk, nut cup filled with peanuts (salted), glass of apple cider, <u>banana cream pie</u>, ala-mode! Doesn't that make your mouth water? Then to add color we had gay little tray napkin with turkeys, etc., and a separate napkin of a different design for ourselves. After Mabel and I had washed etc. in the morning we took turns reading Thanksgiving verses out of the Bible. After dinner we slept and later on had company. We had a very small supper (for which we were very grateful) which consisted of oyster soup (my favorite), coffee cake, ginger cookie, milk, crackers, and peach sauce. Dr. Gorenflo can't tell exactly if I'll have my adhesions cut because it hasn't had time to show yet. But she said my lung is collapsing good.

■ In advanced cases, such as Marilyn's, the lungs could attach themselves to surrounding tissue. If the string-like tissue spread, those adhesions could bind the pleural membranes together, preventing a full collapse.

* * *

Yesterday I got a letter from Agatha Schaus, a letter from Auntie Ruth, and a very cute letter from Mary Lou Conner. Boy but my letters are just stacking up, and I haven't answered a one. Please tell the kids I haven't forgotten them but that I just don't feel like writing yet. I will try to catch up slow but sure.

▪ The "kids" are Marilyn's high school friends. Her letters seem so cheery that they could be coming from a young girl at summer camp. In addition to the adhesions, though, there were indications that she wasn't as well as the tone of her correspondence indicated. The volume of her incoming mail continued to be the talk of the sanatorium, but Marilyn wrote only to her family. She composed her letter first thing in the morning before breakfast arrived, when she felt refreshed by a night's sleep. She napped most of the day, interrupted by meals and nurses.

* * *

Last night Dixie came in with some Christmas wrappings etc., to sell for Ruby Strand. Anyway, Mabel & I bought a 25¢ package together. It had Christmas seals, wrapping paper and ribbon. Very cute for so little. We have planned to decorate our room as much as we can.

▪ Dixie was an orphan from the Minnesota State Public School Orphanage in Faribault, where she developed TB and was transferred to Ah-gwah-ching. Ruby, although confined to bed rest, sold a variety of paper goods from her room. Many magazines and comic books had mail-order advertisements on their back pages offering home-sales opportunities. In sanatoriums, especially those as isolated as Ah-gwah-ching, selling paper goods and beauty notions benefitted both the seller, who needed spending money, and the buyers, who couldn't drive anywhere to buy specialty products. Ah-gwah-ching had a small store that sold necessities, but its stock was limited.

SUNDAY, NOV. 28, 1943

Well, it's exactly a week since you were here. Boy, how time does fly! I can say that now I feel completely rested up from that hectic Monday. Maybe I didn't tell you, but up till now I've done practically nothing but sleep &

more sleep. It was a little too much for me to have all that going on when you were here. Every day my "Wyl Away Diary" has been filled with more and more names. I also have the librarian & teachers on a special page.

▪ The *Wyl Away Diary* was a gift to Marilyn from Helen Gustafson, Aunt Ruth's sister. Helen and her husband lived in Brainerd. The diary, labeled the Hospital Edition, began with a poem about nurses. In a space provided for listing nurses, Marilyn acquired the signatures of Madonna Buter, Emma Sutter, Eleanor Swenson, Florene Reece, Marie Henry, Jessie Smith, Lorrayne Rudd, Hilda Norman, and Sophie White. Another page was for recording gifts; Marilyn listed sixteen things she had received since arriving. Her limited energy was spent on writing letters, however, and the diary was tucked away and forgotten after the initial entries.

* * *

Last nite I was looking over some of the old Moccasins of Mabel's.

▪ Most sanatoriums had an in-house newsletter, and *The Moccasin* was Ah-gwah-ching's. Published monthly "as an educational and recreational project by the White and Indian patients of the Minnesota State Sanatorium," *The Moccasin* was professionally printed and bound in a cover at the Minnesota State Reformatory for Men, commonly known as the St. Cloud Prison. Local copies were five cents monthly or fifty cents a year. Mailed subscriptions were seven cents or seventy-two cents, respectively. Marilyn's arrival was noted in the December 1943 issue. Many sanatoriums exchanged newsletters with each other. One of the trades was with the leper colony near Carville, Louisiana. "We were all in the same boat," said Marilyn, "we were isolated and people were afraid of us."

* * *

P.S. This is to you, Mom. Next time I see you I want you to be just as peppy as your good old self again! An order!! Remember how we used to dance around and laugh & be silly? We're going to do that again someday.

▪ Mothers naturally worry. Mrs. Barnes had more cause to worry than most, and already she was well on her way to losing twenty pounds during the first months of Marilyn's stay at Ah-gwah-ching.

THURSDAY, DEC. 2, 7:30 A.M. (YAWN)
I have quite a bit of news today so wanted to write and give you all the "dirt." Well, for one thing – I'm going to be alone in our room for 3 or 4 days as Mabel is having her operation for adhesions (cut) this afternoon. Dr. Kinsella is here, and Dr. Gorenflo just decided it yesterday. Maybe she'll come back to our room after it, but chances are that she'll be temporarily moved to the BII surgery floor. I won't mind being alone at all because so many people stop in and I have plenty of things to occupy my time.

■ Mabel's adhesions prevented a lung collapse so she had intrapleural pneumonolysis (cauterization) to sever them. The procedure separated the adherent lung from the pleura. The operation was performed by Dr. Thomas Kinsella, a thoracic surgeon. He conquered his own tuberculosis at Cragmor Sanatorium in Colorado Springs. He worked at Glen Lake Sanatorium in Hennepin County from 1925 to 1936 and did several "first" chest surgeries in Minnesota in 1937. Kinsella became an associate clinical professor of surgery at the University of Minnesota and served as a consulting surgeon to many hospitals, including Ah-gwah-ching. Prior to his consultancy, patients traveled to the University Hospital for surgery.

* * *

Miss Reece (you know, charge nurse) has been just lovely to Mabel and I lately. She does extra little things that none of the other nurses do. Now she knows that we behave ourselves she trusts us. Everyone chips in at Christmas and buys the charge, janitor, and cook of our floor a present. I gave 15¢ towards Miss Reece and 10¢ for the others. Miss Reece's present is a beautiful little gold cross on a chain and the janitor – nice shirt, cook – gorgeous hankies.

■ The patients received back rubs twice a day—after breakfast and in the evening before sleep. Some of the nurses really knew how to give back rubs, and Marilyn looked forward to seeing them enter the room. Others would just kind of touch her lightly, and she'd be disappointed. Despite lying in a bed for so long, few patients developed bedsores because of precautions such as back rubs and position changes.

On December 11, Superintendent Callahan wrote a letter to Marilyn's father. In it, he explained that her pleural adhesions were preventing a satisfactory pneumothorax collapse. He thanked Mr. Barnes for signing a permit for surgery, but then he said:

> Maryln [*sic*] is not quite ready for this treatment now. We are gradually increasing her pneumothorax and when the degree of pneumothorax collapse is right we always want to be in a position to proceed without loss of time. Maryln is gaining weight and there has been a material improvement in her symptoms. However, she has developed a small lesion in the upper lobe of her good lung. More adequate treatment of her main lesion should help us to control the new area of disease as well as her original lesion. She was homesick when she first came here, but seems to be much more cheerful and happy now.

Marilyn was unaware of the new development in her right lung.

DEC. 10, 1943, 6:30 A.M. [FRIDAY]

I'm sorry I didn't write some days but am trying to keep the temp down. It's down now to 100° at nite (that's when it's the highest). But in the morning it's always normal. If I just overwork or write too much up it zooms. *Well, now we found out that we* can *have a Christmas tree in our room. Each ward has a big one that is about 7 or 8 ft high and even though we, in the private rooms can buy them, our hall has a big one in it, too. Gary, our janitor, told us yesterday that they also have trees lined up all along the building out a little way on the lawn strung with colored lights so now that I'm by the window (you knew Mabel & I changed beds, didn't you?) I can see it better. I asked the doctor about lessons, and she said not for a couple months. But even if I had started now, in January I probably* couldn't have gotten a credit anyway because it's so late. And health comes before studies.

▓ According to the 1940 census, 68 percent of all adult patients at Ah-gwah-ching did not have a high school diploma. Obtaining a high school diploma or a General Education Development (GED) certificate could help patients prepare for a change in occupation after discharge. Some sanatoriums cooperated with local schools or the state Department of Education to provide opportunities for coursework. Teenagers like Marilyn could take core classes and attempt to keep up with their schoolmates.

SUNDAY AFTERNOON [DECEMBER 12]

I'm so sorry haven't written for a few days but nothing much had happened and I've been writing and sending Christmas cards till I'm blue in the face. Gee, I never realized what work it is, Mom. Thanks so much for the stamps. Boy, I sure needed them and also the Christmas Seals, too. To the people I haven't gotten around to write to I'm writing little notes on the back of the cards so they at least know I'm still thinking of them. Never realized how stationery disappears so fast until now. Especially envelopes! Believe I have some in my old writing portfolio in my room someplace. Anyway that's where I left it when I went to the hospital. Could you find them & bring them up when you come? Mrs. Waddell visited me Friday aft. for the first time and she's just as nice as ever.

▓ Stamp-sized Christmas Seals became the symbol of the National Tuberculosis Association crusade against the disease. Local and state associations sold the Christmas Seals, and ninety-four cents of every dollar raised stayed in the community to pay for anti-tuberculosis activities. People used the stamps to decorate their Christmas cards and gift wrappings.

Marilyn looked forward to seeing her parents, who planned on visiting after Christmas Day. Nola Waddell and her husband, Joseph, lived in Walker. Mr. Waddell was the gardener and groundskeeper at Ah-gwah-ching. He was a shirt-tail relation of Marilyn's mother, his son being married to her first cousin Laura. He was a connection to Marilyn's family, and the couple's visits helped ease her homesickness.

* * *

Rev. Walthers gave the most beautiful sermon last nite. Mabel and I always listen to him through our earphones whenever he speaks. He is going to have a Christmas Day service at 9:30 in the morning and have a program of record Christmas music for ½ hr. Won't that be nice?

■ Marilyn found comfort in her faith. Mabel's minister, the Rev. Paul Walthers, visited members of his Immanuel Lutheran congregation at the sanatorium three times a week. Walthers was of the Missouri Synod, and Marilyn's home church belonged to the Augustana Synod, a difference that mattered to Lutherans of that time. Marilyn noted the similarities in the service but said she would listen to the pastor from the Norwegian synod before deciding with whom she would affiliate. Church services were conducted in the chapel and broadcast through the radio system. Ministers

Ah-gwah-ching's chapel

from various Protestant churches alternated through the month. Catholic Mass was celebrated every other Saturday. Confessions were heard on the first Friday of each month, with distribution of Communion at bedsides the following morning.

* * *

I've gotten "it" since I've been here, but it was about the same as when I was home. Dr. Gorenflo said not to worry about it because it's only natural until I get straightened out.

▪ Marilyn stopped menstruating when she became ill. The female body's response to tuberculosis varied by individual. For some, menstruation stopped for the duration of their illness. Others, like Marilyn, would experience an on-again, off-again cycle with unpredictable flow patterns. Nature seemed to have its own way of coping with sickness and often halted the blood loss a female patient could ill afford.

* * *

Just think! We had 3 <u>men</u> visitors during the afternoon. Only trouble – they're all old enough to be my grandpa! Oh, for some nice <u>young</u> males. But we do enjoy the old guys anyway.

THURSDAY EVE. [DECEMBER 16]

Moms, dear, I'm afraid in my last letter I gave you a very <u>wrong</u> impression.! Really now I wish & wish you wouldn't worry! I happened to mention about Christmas cards and I really only write 2 to 3 a day and just sign my name. In some cases I write a little note but only <u>1</u> a day. And also for the past two weeks or more you folks and you only have gotten letters from me. I did write a penny postal to Ruth also. I haven't been knitting (couldn't get the yarn). Didn't draw or read or anything. Just a little writing everyday and that always in the morning. Honestly, I'm just plain lazy. Eating & <u>sleeping</u> is the main schedule and I do mean sleeping! We sleep from 9-10 in the morn, 12:15 to 2:30 afternoon, 6-7:00 evening & then all night. Boy, if you slept & rested all that time I think you'd be a bit tired of *it, too. I know it's the most wonderful thing for me and I'm doing everything in my power to get home to you as fast as I possibly can. Please believe me! I love you all. I'm sure that the only reason I got so tired out last time you were here was because I was more homesick for you that time, and there were so <u>many</u> of you to talk to at once. Each one of you wanted to talk to me at once and I wanted to listen to everybody. Also I thot it was darn silly to give me pneumo & that crazy running around for the x-rays when my folks were here. It just happened that way, but otherwise I wouldn't have been so all in. Please come up before New Year's, not right after Christmas, but I do want to see you some time during the holidays. I just simply must stop this dreary letter. Reading over it sounds that way.*

■ Although Marilyn tried to allay her mother's fears in this letter, it might have had the opposite effect. Only someone who is seriously ill could be tired enough for three naps and a night's sleep. Also, Marilyn enjoyed drawing and fashion design. She made her own paper dolls and then created clothing for them from wallpaper scraps and bits of lace and rickrack. Her fashion scrapbook had come with her to the sanatorium. For that to lay idle without her drawing in it was not reassuring news.

MONDAY MORN, 7:00 [DECEMBER 20]
I have been feeling fine the last few days and my temp is slowly going down. Just now I took it and it's only 98°. Subnormal, but whose wouldn't be in a cold room in the morning. Last nite our window was open a foot but we're so covered up, all that feels the cold is the cheeks & nose. Last Sat., Miss Reece washed my hair and really, I don't believe it's ever been so clean. She dried it and even washed out my comb and brush just like you used to do, Mother. Last nite she came in and trimmed our windows with red and green strands of that tinsel. Not really tinsel but those kind they used to have in olden times. And then she hung those tinsel icicles down from it. Mr. Waddell brought us a poinsettia so when we put up our Christmas tree, maybe tomorrow or Wed., we'll sure have a pretty room. I am so well

Page from Marilyn's fashion scrapbook

remembered. It makes me feel sort of funny because other people don't get that much. I haven't been hearing from you much this last week. I suppose because the mails are so busy. Nita's letter got here two days after she mailed it. When are you coming up Mom & Daddy? Please come sometime during the holidays because then you can see our decorations & staff. Also, how long do you plan to stay? I'm just awful curious. This week I haven't a thing to do so I'm just going to be lazy and rest up for the holidays. Finished my cards Saturday.

TUESDAY, DEC. 21. 7:00 A.M.

Well, I guess this will be my last letter to you before Christmas or rather the last one you'll get. Oh yes, I made a record yesterday – got 32 cards!! Just darling ones, too. Since yesterday I haven't been doing a thing except reading my mail & listening to the radio. And I'm going to do that and just rest all the rest of this week so I'll be real rested up for Christmas Eve. On that night we have open house and everyone that can walk around (<u>not</u> including <u>us</u>) can visit everyone else in the San. They only do that on special holidays, tho. Well, I think we'll have a good time but my thoughts will be with you all the time. I miss you so but I don't get homesick anymore.

■ Christmas Eve and Christmas Day were happy/sad days for Marilyn. She was pleased to receive an abundance of cards and gifts from friends and family. But when a choir from a church in Walker strolled the halls singing carols, Marilyn wept. She had been in choir at school and church, and she should have been in St. Peter, participating in the usual festivities. Instead, she was bedbound in a sanatorium. She didn't reveal this sadness in her letters to her parents; she continued to be cheery and reassuring.

* * *

Yesterday and today are Miss Reece's days off so we had Smith and Henry for baths. They are both Indians and gosh, they're fun. We laughed more, I got out my Old Spice bath powder & got sprinkled with it for the first time. Mmmm, mmm. Now you can just call me "stinky."
A merry, merry Christmas to all! XXXXX

SUNDAY MORNING, DEC. 26, 1943

Should have written before but I thought I'd wait til I could tell you about my presents and the good time we all had on Christmas Eve. We had fun, but it still didn't seem like Christmas without you folks. I got the most beautiful gifts and everyone stopped in to see us. Mr. Snyder came in and as usual was followed by all his old cronies from Hall Pavilion. I bought some Cokes and we cracked nuts that Mabel's mother sent. We had a swell dinner Christmas

Marilyn and Mabel's first Christmas, 1943

Day. Turkey, dressing, mashed potatoes & gravy, cranberry sauce, apple cider, milk, olives (ripe & green), radishes & celery, & ice cream. Then besides they handed out bags of candy and nuts to everyone. Yesterday Rev. Walthers brought Mabel & I a bag of candy, fruit and nuts like the children at his church got. Also he brought us popcorn balls & beautiful religious calendar for '44. He surely is wonderful to the patients out here.

▩ Marilyn listed the presents she received, including three bed jackets, toilet sets, hair bows, candy, a narcissus plant, a nail polish set with five colors, pajamas, books, war stamps, and jewelry. From her parents she got the chenille bathrobe she had hinted for. Her grandmother gave her a Max Factor makeup kit, and Keith gave her a game. Marilyn got lots of stationery, including two boxes from Helen Gustafson. She later said, "I was loaded with stationery. I didn't know where to put all the boxes. But I used it." Uncle Gerold and Aunt Ruth drove up from Minneapolis to spend Christmas Day with Marilyn. They arrived at 12:30, visited for two hours, and left at 2:30 to get home before dark.

4. A NEW YEAR AND A HEALTH CRISIS

Today I have fluid drained, but it won't be bad

MONDAY [JANUARY 3, 1944]

You'll have to excuse my awful writing as I'm in a terrible position for writing but it's comfortable. Saturday I got the gift Rev. Gustavson spoke of sending. It's a beautiful white cross on a stand and at night or in the dark it shows up. Luminous, you know.

■ The Rev. Eric Gustavson was the minister at Trinity Lutheran Church in St. Peter when Marilyn was confirmed. He had recently moved to New York but sent Marilyn the cross and a booklet, *Meditations and Prayers for the Sick.*

* * *

Haven't done much over the weekend except read. Yesterday morning I had the most gorgeous view from my window. The trees were all frosted & glistening in the morning sun and the snow is so beautiful and white. Today we changed nurses again. They are Mrs. Swenson (one of my favorites), Miss Rudd (she put away my things that first nite I came), Mrs. Arnold (never had her before), Miss Reece, of course, and Mrs. White (the nice Indian nurse who came up to you & talked when you were here last; remember?) Mrs. White is also my personal nurse this month so she'll give me a bath this morning. Boy, I never dreamed a couple of years ago that an Indian would be giving me a bath!

■ Marilyn's life had changed greatly from that of a typical teenager from a small Minnesota town, and that included getting baths from Native nurses. Marilyn signed her letter with a common World

War II greeting, "Keep 'Em Flying." It was the official motto of the US Army Air Corps and its successor, the US Air Force. It was also the title of a 1941 comedy film starring Bud Abbott and Lou Costello and appeared on many war bond and victory posters.

On January 8, Bill Barnes opened a letter from Dr. Gorenflo.

> Dear Mr. Barnes, I am writing to you in regard to your daughter, Marylin [*sic*]. We regret to inform you that Marylin's condition has been worse during the past week. She apparently developed pleural fluid on the left, and an x-ray taken today shows an increased amount of disease in the left lung. The lesion in the right lung appears to be about the same. It will be necessary to postpone her pneumonolysis indefinitely. At the present time, Marylin is running a temperature up to 102 degrees, and appears to have lost weight during the past week. If her condition should become critical, we will notify you by telephone.

Marilyn did not particularly like Dr. Gorenflo and considered her to be lacking in personality. The doctor's matter-of-fact letter seems to be short on empathy for worried parents many miles away from their only daughter. Marilyn had begun to feel very sick. One day she couldn't believe her thermometer—it registered 105 degrees. She tried to read her pulse and couldn't because her heart was beating so fast. She called for the nurse and then became delirious. Her memory of the following days is nonexistent. The disease went into her good lung, and she developed miliary or "galloping" tuberculosis, an infection that arises when bacteria is spread via the body's circulation or lymphatic system. It appears on x-rays as tiny spots; the name is derived from the resemblance to millet grass seed. Miliary TB was often fatal in pre-antibiotic days.

The physicians speculated that the spread started before she came to Ah-gwah-ching, accounting for the lesion that Dr. Callahan had mentioned in his letter. The doctor at St. Peter, thinking Marilyn had pneumonia, treated her with a diathermy machine. Diathermy, a technique that produces hyperpyrexia (high temperature) in the body to promote circulation, had briefly been used in the 1930s to treat lung ailments. Studies regarding the use of diathermy on tuberculosis later found that it warmed the lungs and promoted the bacteria's growth and spread without killing it.[2]

At first, her parents were notified by telephone but told not to come to Ah-gwah-ching. A second phone call prompted Marilyn's mother and Aunt Nita to take the all-day bus trip north. Her father was not able to take time off from his mail route. The women stayed at a small hotel by the lake and walked up to the sanatorium and back. They saw how sick Marilyn was and prayed and prayed for her. Virginia also felt haunted by something that happened when her own aunt, Laura, died when Marilyn was five. Laura had said, "Oh, I wish I could have seen Marilyn when she was sixteen." And Marilyn was now sixteen. Her mother was afraid that she was going to die and be with Laura.

For three long weeks, Marilyn lay in bed while her body gathered the strength to fight off the infection. Marilyn's stationery sat unused; her books unread. Whether it was prayer, genes, or medical intervention, no one can say for sure, but she began to improve. Marilyn's memory of this period is dim, but she remembered one time that Drs. Callahan and Crow stopped at her room. They noticed that the food on her tray was untouched. She told them she had no appetite; the food didn't even look good to her. The doctors scolded her for not eating, and she started to cry. Her nerves were so strained that a harsh word was devastating.

Marilyn's appetite returned, and she resumed her messages home. Although she had a large supply of stationery, her first mailings were on a series of penny postcards preprinted with a one-cent stamp of Thomas Jefferson. Regular envelopes required a three-cent stamp, so the penny postcard saved money for a frequent correspondent like Marilyn. Their small size made them easier for her to hold for writing while lying in bed.

Thursday
Morn.

Dear Folks,
Just a line to
let you know I'm
getting along fine.
(But I still let the
nurses do plenty!)
We've been having
really swell food since
I've been sick. Bananas,
pineapple cake and the
other nite we even
had carmeled apples!
Just like at the fair.
Got the moccasins &
will send them today.
Florence Novak is
going to put my hair
up this morning so
at last — I'll have curls.
Oh Happy Day!!!
Tell Rita not to send
many valentines because
I've bought some more
real cute ones from Dix.
maybe around 8 or 10 she
can send.
So long for now —
All my love — Marily[n]

P.S. I'm really very contented & happy here alone.

One of Marilyn's many postcards to her family

THURSDAY MORN [JANUARY 20]

Just a line to let you know I'm getting along fine (but I still let the nurses do plenty). We've been having really swell food since I've been sick. Bananas, pineapple cake, and the other nite we even had carmeled apples. Just like at the fair. Florence Novak is going to put my hair up this morning so, at last, I'll have curls. Oh Happy Day!

P.S. I'm really very contented & happy here <u>alone</u>.

◾ During Marilyn's illness, Mabel moved to another room.

FRI MORN [JANUARY 21]

Just got thru eating breakfast, and am I full! Sure hope my weight is improving. We get weighed again the 1st of next month. Yesterday I got the most beautiful bouquet of flowers from Mrs. Goodell in Cloquet. Pink long-stemmed carnations with yellow jonquils. Gee, I wish you could see them!

◾ Marilyn's weight sank to eighty-six pounds during her severe illness. She was skeletal, and regaining weight was a struggle for several months. The Goodells were family friends from St. Peter who had recently moved to Cloquet.

MON. MORN [JANUARY 24]

First, I want to thank you for the gorgeous bouquet of snapdragons. They still are just as beautiful today as when they came Fri. Everyone just raves over them. I'm feeling swell and am eating more and more. Yesterday we had turkey dinner topped off with ice cream for dessert. Am going to have my bath and bed made over clean now so better close. Say Hi to everyone and special thank you's to those who sent flowers.

TUES. MORNING, JANUARY 25

Well, how do you like the new stationery? I was just itching to use it but I haven't so much news to write about so this probably won't be so long.

◾ By January 25, Marilyn felt well enough to write a complete letter. She used her new paper from the American Legion Auxiliary with her name printed at the top.

Yes, I got Auntie Ruth's cute puzzle greeting card or rather "get-well" card. Put it together and it's got a cute little kitten in bed on it. Got a nice letter from Roberta and she sure can write nice. Enjoyed it so much.

▨ Roberta Kohl was a friend from high school. On Wednesday, January 26, Marilyn sent a penny postcard that mentioned the weather (fog), ministerial visits (Walthers and Johnson), and an update on Mr. Waddell, who had a hernia operation. Her January 28 postcard reported that she had gone to the lab for an x-ray and blood tests.

SAT. MORN [JANUARY 29]

I asked Dr. Gorenflo yesterday when I could start pneumo again and she said she didn't know for sure but that she was going to aspirate me soon and the regular day for that is Wed. She said a little more fluid had formed since my last x-ray but the amount of fluid in me was small. It doesn't bother my breathing at all anymore.

▨ Marilyn hadn't had a pneumotherapy treatment since her illness because of the adhesions. The accumulation of fluid in the layers between her chest wall and lung signaled yet another change in the ebb and flow of her tuberculosis infection. On January 31, Dr. Callahan mailed a letter to Marilyn's father.

> [Marilyn's] symptoms have been very much better recently and I am very happy to report that her right lung seems to be stabilizing. She has some fluid on the right side and this will have to be aspirated. I think Dr. Gorenflo plans on doing it this week.

Dr. Callahan was incorrect; the fluid was on Marilyn's left, or bad, side.

TUESDAY AFT. [FEBRUARY 1]

I'd like you to come up on either the 12 or 13th or anytime around then convenient. You set the date as I don't know what Rev. G.'s plans are. Haven't written him about coming as I thot you had best plan things out.

▨ The Rev. Herbert Gustafson was the new pastor at Trinity Lutheran Church, where he requested prayers for Marilyn in the
church bulletin. Gustafson used his own car and gas ration points
to bring Marilyn's parents north for a visit.

* * *

*Tomorrow I have fluid drained, but it won't be bad. Almost the same as
pneumo. Mabel may be back with me pretty soon. She seems lots better now.*

▨ Once Marilyn felt better, being alone turned into being lonely.
Mabel had quirky personal habits and nervous tics. They didn't
share many interests, but Mabel was kind and friendly, and they
mostly got along.

THURS. MORN. [FEBRUARY 3]

*Well today I am a very happy gal as my fluid is gone. Yesterday afternoon
I had aspiration and it wasn't so bad. My side is a little sore today from it.*

▨ Marilyn's first aspiration procedure took place in the treatment
room in the building's lower level. The patients waited out in the
hall in their wheelchairs until it was their turn to go in. Marilyn sat
on a chair with the doctor right next to her. An area on her left side
was deadened with Novocain. The doctor inserted a hollow needle
between her ribs into her lung space. The doctor asked Marilyn to
lean into the needle to help her obtain enough pressure to insert it.
Marilyn had a little over one cup of fluid removed, more than 200
cubic centimeters (cc). Being aspirated hurt, but Marilyn didn't
dread having it done because she felt better afterward.

* * *

*Well, Dr. G. promised me a roommate soon. Maybe Kathryn Wells.
Another reason I'm happy is I got another swell letter from Ray Palmer.
Woo! Woo! Am going to send Bob Lavine a Valentine. So you think he likes
me, huh? Gorsh!*

▨ Kathryn Wells was close to Marilyn's age and, from the few
times they had met at treatments, Marilyn believed they would

be compatible as roommates. Ray Palmer was Marilyn's pen pal in London, connected through the *Child Life* club. Bob Lavine and his father were active in Boy Scouts at St. Peter, where Marilyn's father had established the first troop. Marilyn had a crush on Bob before she left for the sanatorium, but he was shy.

FRIDAY MORN. FEB. 4TH

I'm still feeling good and last night slept the best since I've been sick. Last nite (5:40) I got a cute joint letter from Sharyn and her girlfriend Deborah. Mory also wrote a line and sent some photos of Sharyn and him. Now for that list of things I'd like. 1. Photograph album (it was in my room the last so you probably know where it is). 2. Envelope of photo negatives of pictures I've taken (in a lower left pigeonhole in Daddy's desk). 3. The watch. 4. I sure would like it if you could bring some ginger ale and fruit juices. I just crave it. Every afternoon I have a mixed drink. Doesn't that sound terrible?

▉ Marilyn's uncle Mory managed the J.C. Penney store in St. Peter and Salet's Department Store in North Mankato before moving to Arizona later in life. Sharyn was his daughter. Marilyn stashed ginger ale and other nonperishable food items on top of the locker in her room. On Saturday morning, Marilyn sent another postcard listing more items she wanted her family to bring. She said, "I'll write more tomorrow as space is short." When "tomorrow" arrived, Marilyn didn't write because she had another aspiration. She also gained a roommate, Martha Schrodt, on Saturday.

5. ROOMMATES

I'm getting so lonesome

MONDAY NIGHT [FEBRUARY 7]

I'm feeling swell and my temp is normal all the time. But best of all I'm eating just like my old self again and in fact, I seem to enjoy the food so much more. Whether it's the food or me, I don't know. Boy, I sure have my "roommate troubles." This lady is still here because they didn't give her an exam today, and they don't know where to move her until they find out her condition. She is 30 yrs old and has 3 children and another one on the way. Imagine!! I've never seen such a pessimistic character – there's something wrong with everything. Honestly, I could just scream! And just when I'm beginning to enjoy life again. But this morning when she was gone for x-ray etc. I talked with Mrs. Swenson who is charge nurse here now, and she said that she'd see she'd be moved, and I could be alone when you folks come. She's just a peach of a nurse and almost a mother to me up here.

■ Martha Schrodt and her husband did indeed have three children, ages eight, seven, and two, whom she would not be able to see, except through a window, for an extended period of time. Tuberculosis and pregnancy put a double strain on her system, and no one could predict whether her baby would be tuberculous when born.

* * *

Today I got the cutest picture letter from Mory.

■ Uncle Mory enjoyed illustrating letters and envelopes with cartoonish figures. Most represented people he knew; some letters were in story form.

* * *

On the envelope:

After 5 days, return to
M.W. LAUMANN
907 E. 1ST ST.
FAIRMONT, MINNESOTA.

RUSH

C Ⅱ

Miss MARILYN BARNES
STATE SANITARIUM
AH-GWAH-CHING
MINNESOTA

UNITED STATES POSTAGE 3 CENTS

**Envelope decorated
by Marilyn's uncle Mory**

This afternoon Mabel asked the doctor for permission to stop in for a visit with me after pneumo. And to her and my surprise she said yes! So Mabel came and we had the best visit. Seemed so darn good having somebody your own age again to talk with. You know, she finished that doily and is going to sell it for $1.75. (Here's a secret – she only paid 15¢ for material). They sure go like hot-cakes, too.

▨ Mabel's doily was part of occupational therapy at Ah-gwah-ching, which was based primarily on craft work. The instructor at the time of Marilyn's stay was Martha Emig, who was hired in 1934. Only patients who were improving in health and could sit up in their beds participated. Projects for women consisted of home crafts such as sewing, embroidery, tatting, crocheting, and knitting. Many of the men did leatherwork. Some who learned woodworking at the sanatorium became carpenters or made furniture after their discharge. Although the craft work was meant to keep patients busy, they could earn money by selling their products in the Occupational Therapy Shoppe or at other venues, including fairs. Beadwork and dolls were especially encouraged for the Native patients, who could sell their work through trading posts near tourist resorts.

THURS. MORN [FEBRUARY 10]

Well, I had my exam Tues. and didn't find out much from Dr. Gorenflo. Also, I wouldn't be taking pneumo again until my fluid starts diminishing. I'm sort of peeved at the doctor because she won't move this roommate & I don't like her. I'm going to write a note to Mrs. Swenson today and ask her to ask the Dr. to do something about this so I can be alone on Monday. But just in case she's still here when you come you be sure and persuade the doctor to move her. If I don't get a steady roommate soon, the doctor said I'll have to expect getting new people when they come in because they're short of room. I want Mabel back because I see now how lucky I was when I had her.

■ It had taken some time for Marilyn, who had a bedroom to herself at home, to adjust to the roommate situation with Mabel. Mabel's health was improving, however, and she would move to Building B if her progress continued. Rejoining Marilyn now would result in two relocations instead of one.

FRIDAY MORN. [FEBRUARY 11]

Well, my roommate is still here so it looks like she'll be here on Mon. Today is Mrs. Soper's birthday so I am going to send her a Valentine I made myself. I've been making a few and everyone just raves over them.

■ Rose Soper was from Mankato, not far from St. Peter, and Marilyn befriended her as a person to talk to about home.

* * *

Yesterday, Mrs. White (Indian) washed my hair for the first time since Dec. 18 and last nite Florence Novak came over and put it all up for me.

■ Patients on strict bed rest had their hair shampooed every two weeks, but it had been almost two months since Marilyn's last shampoo. In the meantime, talcum powder had been combed through her hair to remove some of the oil.

* * *

P.S. Could you please get me lead for my Eversharp, Daddy?

Marilyn wrote with a mechanical pencil so that she didn't have to worry about sharpening a regular pencil. The roommate situation so irritated Marilyn that a few hours after mailing her morning postcard she wrote another one that returned to the subject.

FRIDAY AFT.

This roommate is still here, and Dr. Gorenflo doesn't do a thing about it. I'm so mad! But everyone tells me not to get Mabel back so I don't know what to do. You'll have to help me when you come.

SAT. MORN. [FEBRUARY 12]

Hope you get this tomorrow but if you don't it won't matter much, I guess. Just wanted to tell you about the little party we had last nite. Mrs. Soper had a birthday and she gave everyone on our floor a cute little nut cup filled with heart candy and a cupcake with a candle in the center. This was on our supper tray and we had a good supper also. Each got a whole banana.

Marilyn's parents visited her on Sunday.

WED. AFTERNOON, FEB. 16, 1944

I went for aspiration this aft but she said there wasn't enough today to take off. Boy was I glad! I'm not in the least tired today. Had a good nap this afternoon, too. Well, now I'm alone again and I think I'll have a pal again soon. I was surprised they moved Mrs. Schrodt so soon. She went to the B building, and I guess Mabel will be going there, too. Everyone (the nurses and patients) tells me what nice folks I have and they sure wouldn't have had to tell me either. I found that out long ago.

FRIDAY MORN. [FEBRUARY 18]

Well I'm still alone in my room but maybe will have someone soon. I hope! Gee have they ever been moving the people around. They moved Florence & Margaret over to BIII yesterday, and I'm just sick over it. Mabel may be moved to BII any day now so it looks like I'm the only young one left here. Now there are 2 vacant rooms on this floor & 4 rooms with only 1 patient in it.

FEBRUARY 19, 1944 [SATURDAY]

I'm still alone but I'm <u>patiently</u> waiting for a bed pal. Miss Willsie, the lady nurse you met on the bus, stopped in a bit tonite. I like her a lot and hope she comes on CII next month. Just got through listening to "Inner Sanctum Murder Mysteries" on the radio. Brrr – are they ever gory things. I just love the way he says, "Pleasant dreams" at the end of the show and then shuts the squeaky door. Did you listen tonight? By the way, I got a nice letter from Jimmy Wieland yesterday, and I guess he thinks I'll be home pretty soon to go to shows in Kato again with him. Ha! But boy, I only wish that was true. I've gotten to be contented here though and trained myself not to wish for things I know can't be possible.

■ Jimmy Wieland, of Le Sueur, had been Marilyn's first real date. They went to a movie in Mankato when she was about fifteen, but there hadn't been a second date.

* * *

Well, so long for now folksies. I hear the delightful clang and clatter of "the bed pan parade."

■ The "bed pan parade," like any other parade, was preceded by the sound of crashing cymbals every evening when the clean pans were distributed. The stacks of metal bedpans bouncing on a metal cart made a lot of noise. Patients on strict bed rest used bed pans. Marilyn used one for two years. They were kept in a cold closet, and in winter the nurses would sometimes put hot water in them to warm them up.

WEDNESDAY MORNING [FEBRUARY 23]

Seems so good to be writing with ink again and this pen is slick!

■ Previously, Marilyn had to lie flat in bed to rest. As her temperature remained normal, the head of her bed was raised so that she could do more things for herself. When flat, she had to write with a pencil, but she preferred to use a fountain pen.

* * *

Yesterday I got a note from Mrs. Schrodt on BII and she says she has a nice roommate 26 years old and likes it fine there. Hope I get as good a match.

■ The animosity between Marilyn and her former roommate disappeared once Mrs. Schrodt was out of their room. Looking back at the experience with her "bad" roommate, Marilyn acknowledged that she was too immature then to understand the stress of being pregnant in a sanatorium and worrying about children at home.

THURSDAY, FEBRUARY 24TH

This morning I got a package in the mail from Grandma B and Aunt Mary. They sent me some yummy chocolate covered wafers, a Hershey bar, and some more Toll House chocolates. I sure would love some of the cookies you make from it, because Toll House are my favorite and they don't spoil easy. Don't send any very soon please as I still have Grandma's to finish.

■ Grandma B was widowed when Marilyn's father was only twelve. Nellie Barnes lived with her daughter Mary Latch in Iowa but spent part of the year visiting her son Leon and his wife, Stella. She stayed with Bill's family every summer. Toll House cookies were still a relative novelty in 1943 and had not yet acquired the more generic name of chocolate chip cookies. They were invented in 1936 at the Toll House Inn at Whitman, Massachusetts, when cut-up pieces of a Nestlé chocolate bar were added to plain cookie dough. Nestlé began selling ready-made chips in 1939.

I had aspiration again yesterday and she took off a little over a cup. It didn't seem to hurt as much yesterday either. I was in an almost sitting up position. Boy, but did I sweat! It's just the nervousness everybody goes through, I guess. I still haven't the slightest idea when I get a roommate. Gosh, I do hope it's soon because I'm getting so lonesome and lately hardly anyone comes to visit. Then, too I can't find so much to keep me busy as when there are two.

SATURDAY MORN. [FEBRUARY 26]

Well, yesterday I got my hair washed again by Mrs. White as she didn't get all the soap out last time. I went in the wheelchair again – the 1st time after my sickness. I also weighed myself in the bathroom and I've gained 4 lb in the last 2 weeks. Now I have only <u>20</u> more to go to be back to my last summer's weight. Whew! We have a new nurse on the floor – the sister of our librarian & is she swell! Real jolly & never gets crabby.

■ The library at Ah-gwah-ching was established in 1908, with donations of 250 books from women's clubs in St. Paul and Minneapolis. The library collection grew, and Rachel Rothnem was hired as a full-time librarian in 1934. Her sister, Ragna, had previously worked at the state's School for the Feeble Minded in Faribault.

SUNDAY MORNING [FEBRUARY 27]

I noticed Bill Gessner is going to be drafted now pretty soon. That's too bad. Gee, but it seems like so many of our St. Peter boys are 'missing in action' or killed. Yesterday a sack of oranges and two candy bars was left at the office for me and the card read – "Mrs. Stoffregen & Doris." I have heard that name before but just can't place who they are. Please let me know. So now I have a dozen oranges to eat. But how I love 'em.

■ Bill survived the war. The Stoffregens farmed in Nicollet County, and they sent the sack of treats to Marilyn via neighbors who were visiting a sister at the sanatorium—an act of kindness from people Marilyn barely knew. On Tuesday morning, Marilyn sent a postcard lamenting the lack of anything to do. She hoped the librarian would be making rounds. The Ah-gwah-ching librarian visited patients' rooms with a book cart that was custom-made at the sanatorium. The top shelf pivoted left or right, so a bed patient could easily select a book.

THURSDAY MORN 6:00 A.M. [MARCH 2]
I have just finished washing, etc. so will use this time before breakfast to write. Yesterday I went down for aspiration and had the best visit with Betty Carlson and Kathryn Wells. Then when Dr. G. did fluoroscope me she said I could go back upstairs again as she wouldn't aspirate today. I was so glad. Now I think I'll be on a 2 wks schedule.

▓ Fluoroscopy is basically using an x-ray machine to obtain a "real-time" look at a lung. For a pneumotherapy procedure, the doctor learned the shape and position of the collapsed lung before

Library book cart custom-made for bed patients

introducing additional air. Dr. Gorenflo used fluoroscopy before aspiration to see whether the shadow indicating fluid in Marilyn's lung had grown. Fluoroscopy was popular because it was non-invasive, and it was relatively inexpensive because the image was not saved to a plate. Marilyn was fluoroscoped every two weeks for more than a year, and she had an x-ray every three months. In later years, once the link to cancer became known, she refused any unnecessary radiation, even for her teeth. She knew that she was already over-radiated. A 1991 research study found that 2,573 women treated for tuberculosis between 1925 and 1954 were examined by x-ray fluoroscopy an average of eighty-eight times during therapy. The researchers found "strong evidence for a linear relationship between doses and breast cancer risk." Breast tissue is especially susceptible to radiation injury, with young women at the most risk. Marilyn was told that she was also at elevated risk for leukemia. She was fortunate to have escaped those consequences during her lifetime.[3]

* * *

Yesterday I showed my bum toe to Dr. Callahan & he called it a "drop toe." I got neuralgia in it when I was so toxic during my sickness, he said. But it'll come back when I get well.

■ At some time during Marilyn's illness, a branch of her peroneal nerve was compressed or damaged, resulting in her big toe's "drop."

SATURDAY MORN. [MARCH 4]

Yesterday Olga was over and I bought a necklace from her that she crocheted. It was $1 but I thot I'd get it for a present for someone as she has been so nice & is going to let me have her mattress.

■ Olga Hultberg was about thirty-five years old and had been in the sanatorium for several years. She grew up in one of the towns affected by the 1918 Cloquet fire. She worked in her father's store, and they survived the fire by standing in a pond holding the store's cashbox. Olga had a mattress to sell because of a quirk in the sanatorium's purchasing system. Ah-gwah-ching was originally administered by the State Board of Control, which governed the state's mental and penal institutions. The sanatorium's furnishings were obtained under those institutional purchasing contracts. Patients on continuous bed rest were lying on the same thin cotton mattresses as prison inmates. Thus, a market for innerspring mattresses developed within the sanatorium. Patients would buy their own or obtain a used one from a discharged patient. Staff would steam-clean a mattress and give final approval before allowing it to be reused. Just prior to Marilyn's arrival, the sanatorium had been placed under the directorship of the Minnesota Department of Welfare's Division of Social Welfare. Not until 1946 was Dr. Callahan's request for funds finally approved, and seventy-six innerspring mattresses were purchased at a cost of $1,195.48.

* * *

Yesterday afternoon Harriet Peterson gave me her new Wards catalogue, and I've picked out a pair of play shoes I'd like to get. They'd be just swell for when I do go in the wheelchair & before long I hope to be up a little more. Do you think I might get them? They are $4.95.

6. SETTLING IN

Now I have some hope

MARCH 5 SUNDAY MORN

At the end of the month we usually change nurses but this month we're not. All the same ones except Katherine Day (Indian) because she quit and a nice white girl – Doris Olsen is taking her place. Yesterday I got a swell pile of mail as I usually do every Saturday. During the week I only get from 1 to 3 letters or cards, but Saturdays bring 4, 5, or 6. Mabel got permission to come over for about an hour yesterday, and it sure seemed good to have little chat. But I sure wouldn't want her as steady diet. She's still just as <u>silly</u> as ever.

MONDAY NITE, MARCH 6, 1944

Don't you feel honored that I'm writing two letters in a row! Yes, I'm in a good mood for writing with the wind and snow howling outside my window. I had my bath this morning & weekly house cleaning and I have a new "personal" nurse. Instead of Mrs. White, it's Miss Arnold. She's just swell and is real thorough like Miss Reece. She's very nice to talk with too. She's had a lot more training than these nurses' aides. Not a registered nurse, but what they call a "T.B. Graduate."

■ "TB-graduate" nurses helped to address the nursing shortage at many sanatoriums. Usually they were practical nurses who had taken a course on tuberculosis and completed a short internship at a sanatorium or TB hospital.

* * *

On the subject of nurses – Miss Hilda Norman is now in the Navy. She was sworn into the WAVES last Friday and she leaves for some college in N.Y. April 18th. Then after her boot training she will be stationed in a hospital in California. Hilda's so excited over it and I sure don't blame her. Gladys (Nimps) Hanson came over yesterday afternoon and Ethel in the evening to tell me they are going home in a week and a half or two weeks. Boy, how I envy those girls.

■ The Nimps sisters were originally from St. Peter. Gladys was a nurse, and Ethel was a patient who later worked as an aide.

* * *

I'm sending for those shoes tomorrow and had Miss Arnold help me fill out the order blank and money order. I could use a dollar or two if you can spare as 5 dollars takes quite a hole out of your pocket. My remaining amount of cash on hand is $1.23.

■ Marilyn also asked her parents for an electric popcorn popper. On March 7, Marilyn's mother wrote to share family news—and also to suggest that Marilyn write to Warren Wetherill or some other soldiers who needed a cheering letter: "You write so well everyone enjoys your letters." She added a postscript, "If time goes by too slowly, why don't you write a book? Keep a diary?"

WEDNESDAY AFT. MARCH 8, 1944

I just came from aspiration and I'm oh so happy I just had to sit down and write you a letter. You see today Dr. Gorenflo was away for some reason so Dr. Callahan aspirated. Well, the first thing to make me happy was that I went in the wheelchair for the first time and walked. I am no longer a <u>cart</u> patient. Wheeee! Then I talked with Kathy Wells and Betty Carlson and Erna Hahn and we were wondering why Dr. G. wasn't there. We all got the jitters when they said Callahan would take her place because he might not be as gentle as we were used to. I was the first one in too, but, gee, he's swell. I'm just crazy about Callahan, and he was even gentler than Gorenflo. When he first looked at my lung with the fluoroscope he remarked how *much I've improved since he saw my last x-ray. He said my lung is collapsed so much better and I'm coming along fine. That sure was music to my ears. I surely don't see why Dr. Gorenflo can't say some nice things when there's nice things to say. But I guess she'll always be a clam! Boy, my morale is about 100% higher. Now I have some hope. Yesterday I got the corniest letter from Uncle Mory. Honestly! How I laughed. He addressed the envelope Miss Marilyn [drawing of a barn]s and then had a lot of other funny drawings on it. I sure enjoy his letters. They cheer me up so.*

P.S. It was 18 below this morning here. And my window was wide open all night! Glad to have my cozy Hudson Bay blanket!!

■ Marilyn's wool blanket with its red, green, and yellow stripes had been purchased during a trip to International Falls and Fort

**Dr. Francis Callahan, Ah-gwah-ching
superintendent in the 1940s**

Francis when she was three years old. The blanket was yet another link to home. In a postcard sent Monday, March 13, Marilyn summarized her mail and described a patient's birthday party.

WED. MORN. 7:30 A.M. [MARCH 15]
Well, I have some news for you – Mabel was moved over to BII yesterday morning and I didn't even know it until last nite when Elsie stopped by and told me. She's in an alcove off the porch and all alone too. Will go down for aspiration again today and am going to wear my new shoes. The novelty of wearing my new robe hasn't worn off yet either so I sure get a kick out of "dressing up." This will be the fourth time I've ever worn it.

▪ Even "toe drop" didn't stop Marilyn from wearing her new shoes. She had to hold her toe up and quickly put her shoe on. It didn't always work on the first try, but the joy of sitting in a wheelchair and having her feet show was worth the effort.

THURSDAY MORNING [MARCH 16]
Got your box of things in the mail yesterday and thanks so much. I sure will enjoy eating the delicious cookies and Saturday nite will probably pop some corn as Dorothy Reetz is coming over to knit with me. Also a new girl I met, Lucille Larson – about my age. They both are real nice girls from DII wards. Last nite I visited with the daughter of that real sick old lady next door to me. She said her mother, Mrs. Rither, is failing terribly now and they think she'll go in about 2 weeks. Also Hannah Smith, another old lady, is dying I guess. So we'll have some more empty beds. The floor seems quite empty already with Mabel, Florence & Margaret moved. I'm getting awfully lonesome without some people my own age. All the young kids are on BII & III.

▪ Marilyn had been alone in the room for one month.

THURSDAY NITE, 7:30 P.M. [MARCH 16]
Today I only got one lonesome little letter but one is better than nothing I guess. Here is some local news. Dallas Skary [Skare] ("Gary") our janitor

is today the proud papa of an 8 lb new baby boy. Everyone congratulated him this morning and this afternoon Mrs. Millark [Millarch] went around with a card to sign and everyone gave $.10 toward a gift for the baby. They always do nice things for our help. Olga just was over and we had a nice little talk until the bed pans scared her away. She says to greet you from her.

[LETTER CONTINUED ON ST. PATRICK'S DAY, MARCH 17]

Boy oh boy, was I ever showered with mail today. I got 10 letters. Ruth Johnson sent me 12 three-cent stamps. That was the best of all. I just used up my last card & stamp today too.

MONDAY MORNING [MARCH 20]

Am sort of sleepy this morning as I woke up several times in the night and couldn't get back to sleep because of that sick lady's groaning and moaning next door. It's a pity she can't pass away and stop her suffering. She's 80 years old so she's lived her life. It sure is gruesome to have to be here with no young kids and all those old sick people. The other floors are nothing but "happy" all the time (especially DII, BII, & BIII). If I had a chance to move to BII or III I'd sure move in a minute if I didn't like the location of my room so well. Everyone says it's nice – so sunny and I'll have an advantage this summer.

THURSDAY [MARCH 23]

I went down for aspiration yesterday but she said there wasn't enough formed again so it'll be 3 weeks without having aspiration. Mrs. Rither died. That makes 5 since I've been here. I talked to Dr. Gorenflo about being so lonesome and she answered me <u>frankly</u> for the first time. She said she has been on the lookout for a roommate but there just isn't anyone my age. She said that when I get a little strong I can move to the BII Porch. Oh, I'd sure love that and so many young people over there. She also said I could take lessons soon. Mrs. White quit or something so now we have Gladys (Nimps) Hanson on the floor. Gee it's swell. She comes to "visit" me a lot now.

■ Leora Rither, seventy-two, died on the twenty-first. The other patient, Hannah Smith, passed away two days earlier. More than twenty people had died in the entire sanatorium since late October, but Marilyn was probably aware of only those in her building. When a patient died, the nurses shut all the doors on the floor, but the patients could still hear the cart coming down the hall to get the body and take it to the morgue. After the deceased had been removed, the nurses would open up the doors, but they wouldn't talk about the death. Marilyn said the patients themselves talked very little about death. They tried to not dwell on that possibility and instead celebrated improvements in their health. The undertaker at the funeral home in Walker was Earle Thomas, and he collected most of the bodies, wearing a mask and taking other precautions while embalming. The deceased would usually be transported to their hometown, and most people who died at Ahgwah-ching were buried in family plots. Sometimes the deceased was a transient or the family could not afford the cost of transport. Those patients were buried in a section of Evergreen Cemetery in Walker that was designated for sanatorium use. During Marilyn's three years at the sanatorium, 162 patients died.

MARCH 25, 1944, [MARILYN WROTE TO HER BROTHER KEITH]
While I'm writing this letter to you now, you're probably still snoozing in bed as it is now exactly 7:15 in the morning. Since it is Saturday and you don't have to go to school, I'll bet you are going to have a swell day out playing marbles or roller skating in this nice Spring weather. Sure wish you could come along next time [when the parents visit] *but I think in June it would be nicer. Then I might be able to see you outside instead of just looking through a window. I miss you a lot, Keith, but I'm planning to come home next Christmas for a 2-week visit. It's a long way off but won't that be fun? Mr. Snyder, an old man from St. Peter also comes to see me every Saturday afternoon & one time he was telling me about a cute little squirrel*

outside they call "Oscar." He is so tame he'll run right up on your shoulder
& dig in your pockets for something to eat. Imagine that.

■ Keith received his letter on Saturday afternoon, and on Sunday
their mother wrote to Marilyn about it: "He was so happy & proud
to get one from you and, of course, we all enjoyed it." She noted
that Marilyn sounded "peppy" and more like her old self again.

WED MORN. [MARCH 29]

Gee, is it ever beautiful outside this morning. The frost & snow makes every
tree & bush look like white lace. I sure would love to be out walking in the
snow today. My new mattress is "just like heaven" unquote. Really, it's just
like my bed at home now. Please thank Mrs. Ritt [a family friend] *for the*
cards and stamps. That sure was swell.

THURSDAY MORNING [MARCH 30]

I got all dressed up in my shoes and housecoat & went down again yester-
day but didn't have to be aspirated <u>again</u>*. Now it'll be a month since I've*
had it. Do you suppose you could bring along my pink blouse that buttons
down the back & a pair of my rayon panties? My snuggies are too itchy
and hot to wear under heavy slacks. Ethel Nimps came over last night and
she is going to wash out my pajamas and a pair of socks for me.

■ Marilyn's "snuggies" were underwear made partly of wool. The
panties came down to about mid-thigh, and a vest-like top had
straps over the shoulders. They were very warm for winter but irritated her skin.

APRIL 2ND, 1944 [SUNDAY]

Surprise! I have another roommate. Yes, just this morning they moved a
new lady in with me and I like her real well. Her name is Mrs. Irene Lahti
from Cloquet, Minn. She has 5 children and is Lutheran. She's very easy
to get along with and I do enjoy having company once more even though
it isn't a girl my own age. "Irene" as she wants me to call her, doesn't have

much trouble if at all and she probably will get some privileges right away. *They caught it in the really early stages. She's so different than Mrs. Schrodt in her attitude in coming here. She never complains and tries to like every-thing and isn't homesick. I think we'll get along fine.*

▨ Marilyn had been alone in her room since February 15. Irene Hill Lahti was thirteen years older than Marilyn and was another pregnant roommate with children at home.

* * *

We've gotten 5 new patients in since last week. Tomorrow we change nurses again and Miss Willsie, the nurse you met on the bus, is going to be on this floor. I'm so glad. I just heard that Mrs. Swenson, our charge nurse is expecting. That means that we'll be having a new charge again soon. I'm so anxious to see you and you can't imagine how happy I was to hear you are coming for Easter Sunday and will stay more than a day. Only I sure wish Gram & Keith could come as long as you're coming by car. Will be seein' you soon.

p.s. I've just about run out of popcorn now. Hint! Hint!

▨ The culture of the time expected that a pregnant woman did not work. Mrs. Swenson gave up her job as charge nurse.

7. SPRING 1944

Haven't done much but sleep

MONDAY MORNING [APRIL 3]

Gosh, I feel so nice and cozy in my warm room looking out at snow falling gently. Ah, Spring! It brings out the poet in me. Something has happened over the week end. Guess what? I've got a terrible "crush" on a boy here & have I got it bad! Have you heard the Song – "It's Love, Love, Love"? Well, my heart went bumpity bump & my knees went knockety knock when I first met him Sat. afternoon (Please excuse all this boring "mush") To go on – He's known as "Bex" around here. His real name is Marshall Lee Bex, and he's from Walker. Bex is 18 and had just been in the U.S. Maritime Service a short time before he found out he had T.B. He came here in December and isn't very sick as he goes visiting Saturdays. Gosh but he's cute.

■ The Moccasin's profile of Bex said he had been stationed at Sheepshead Bay, Brooklyn, New York, when he became ill.

* * *

You should see me primp nowadays. You won't know the old gal next time you see me. Well, one thing I'm getting out of this ordeal is some time to take care of my hair, nails, etc. I was awfully lonesome for all of you folks yesterday. It seemed everyone had company from home on our floor except me. But then I'll have you at Easter. Now even the full privileged patients can't come and visit other nites but Sat. unless they have a special pass from their doctor so won't see many kids during the week. They're getting so darn strict. That's one reason why I want to move to BII where so many kids are.
Lots of Lingering Love,
Lynn (I feel more like a "Lynn" today instead of Marilyn)

◾ Lynn was not a name that Marilyn used at home in St. Peter, although she had always liked it. She decided she wanted to be called Lynn at Ah-gwah-ching, and she began signing her name that way to some of her pen pals. Perhaps it was a way to cope with having an often-fatal illness: Lynn experiencing the sanatorium stay instead of Marilyn. She continued to sign "Marilyn" in most letters to her family, but articles in *The Moccasin* referred to her as Lynn.

TUESDAY AFTERNOON, 4 O'CLOCK [APRIL 4]

Please thank Miss Miller for the money. I remember her quite well. She always has such pretty peonies and I remember when we used to sneak apples from that big tree right near the side walk. I never told you but one time I ate a whole lot of green ones when Roberta & I were "just kids." Boy, those were the good old days. Yes, I got your $2 last week and I've already had use for it. My toe still doesn't move much but I think it's a little better. It has turned the most beautiful purple right on the 1st joint. Gosh, all colored up for Easter. My cough is sure improved. I hardly cough at all anymore and don't use the sputum cup enough to need it. I'm so glad. That terrible coughing around Christmas just wore me out. My cravings have passed away to a certain extent, and I hardly eat candy any more. What I like best is to have a good candy bar now & then. So if you happen to fall upon some good ones like milk chocolate Hershey, Bit o' Honey, Love Nest, Baby Ruth, Milky Way, etc., I'd appreciate having some. They are always out of them here and when they do get any the people up and around nab them.

WED. NITE [APRIL 5]

I'm very sorry to report to you that my "crush" has come to an all-too-sudden end! Bex goes home tomorrow for good. He really didn't have T.B., just fluid.

◾ Misdiagnoses happened. The symptoms of bronchiectasis, emphysema, and the early stages of lung cancer were similar to those

of tuberculosis. Marshall Lee Bex might have had a non-TB myco-
bacterial infection.

* * *

▦ Marilyn's parents visited on Easter Day, Sunday, April 9.

WEDNESDAY MORN. [APRIL 12]

*Here I am again! Irene & I sure have been taking it easy lately. Gee, we
sleep practically <u>all</u> day. But I wasn't so tired after you left. Irene taught me
how to crochet yesterday afternoon so as soon as I can get a pattern I'll start
the pot holders. I was just looking over my pajamas and those blue ones
Nita gave me have some plastic buttons that are falling apart so could you
send up some good substantial white buttons (not plastic).*

▦ Patients complained about the condition of their clothing. Hot
wash water faded colors, and the use of mangles for ironing destroyed buttons and decorations. Anything delicate, such as lace
or fine fabric, rarely survived for long in the sanatorium laundry.
Female patients who were on exercise often hand-washed such
items for other patients.

* * *

▦ Marilyn's postcard on Saturday, April 15, reported: *Irene and I
have been so lazy, and it seems we haven't done much but sleep.*

SUNDAY MORNING [APRIL 16]

*It's a nice sunny day today but so dull around here. A lot different from
last Sunday. Irene is sort of blue today. I've been reading and crocheting.
Also knitting. Went in on Olga's paper group at 12¢ a month so are getting
the Star Journal daily and Sunday. Today we had steak and chocolate ice
cream. Miss Rothnem brought me a second dish and I ate it. Wow! Am
I full. Here is a list of things I'd like you to send next week if you can: 1.
Pink blouse, 2. Panties (silk), 3. Listerine, 4. Buttons for pajamas (white),
5. Tape measure, 6. New summer pajamas (if you can buy some.)*

▦ Marilyn later said, "One thing I thought when I reread my letters is that I was rather selfish in that I expected my parents to send me stuff all the time. I thought, 'My gosh, I ask for so much all the time.' Those were kind of thin times. My folks didn't have an excess of funds." But she was a sixteen-year-old girl. There was no large town nearby for shopping even if she could go out, and the sanatorium store stocked only necessities.

APRIL 19, 1944, WEDNESDAY
I've been working on my crocheting quite a bit, but today am going to read magazines we got from the library – Cosmopolitan, American, and 2 Time magazines. I am going to send my rayon pajamas home for you to wash and iron too if I can find a box today. I asked the nurse about it and she said if you hang them outside in the sun for 6 hours it disinfects them enough.

■ The efficacy of sunshine as a disinfectant was debated for centuries. Researchers discovered that direct, unfiltered sunlight, particularly the violet end of the spectrum, killed tuberculosis bacteria. This knowledge gave rise to heliotherapy: a TB treatment that had near-naked patients taking sunbaths. Eventually it was discovered that heliotherapy was most effective on bone TB. In the pulmonary cases, sunlight raised the body's temperature and provided warm moisture in the lungs on which the bacteria thrived.[4]

SAT. AFTERNOON [APRIL 22]
This is the first rain since Easter so everyone is really enjoying it way down to the birds & squirrels and little bits of green grass peeping through. Nothing much new except I took a little walk last night to the new patient next door and stayed about 10 minutes and then jumped into bed again. Feels so good to get up & stretch your limbs once in a while. Irene isn't feeling so hot today. Got pains in her tummy but I'm swell as usual.

■ Marilyn's unauthorized walk was against the rules of her strict bed rest, but she and her roommates would sometimes get out of bed when the door was closed for rest hour, just for the sensation of being upright. Other patients sneaked out of bed, too, for short visits with her.

MONDAY EVENING [APRIL 24]

We had our baths today and I put on my new pajamas. Gee, it seems funny to have drawstring pants! Saturday we got another new patient and she's just about my age, I think. Her last name is Fraiser [Swaser] and she's in with Clara because all the other rooms are filled up. I'm going to try to get acquainted but it's pretty hard – both being strict bed. Well, I guess that's all for now. Got to get ready for bed. Get ready for bed! Ha! That's a laugh.

FRIDAY MORN [APRIL 28]

I've just torn myself away from the May basket production line in order to write my faithful note. I received the May Day package from Grams and Nita yesterday and we lunched on the delicious stullen bread for dinner. Tell them thanks <u>so much</u>! Also, for the gum & blue flowers. They are really something up here as we don't have anything like that this early.

■ Stullen (stollen) is a buttery, dense yeast bread made with dried fruit, nuts, and spices. The blue flowers were little dogtooth violets that grew in the ravines between St. Peter and Mankato. It was a Barnes family tradition to gather them for May baskets.

SATURDAY [APRIL 29]

Another surprise! I'm once again "a lone wolf." Irene got terrible cramps yesterday noon and was real sick so Dr. Gorenflo & Mrs. Swenson moved her in another room so she could be alone. It seems so lonesome without her but maybe she'll come back again. I hope so. It's another dreary day today and oh, how I <u>hate</u> 'em. I'm going to visit Yvonne & Harriet either this afternoon or night. Dr. G. said I could go right away after I asked her. Didn't have to <u>wheedle</u>! Hope I hear some good news at my exam next week. P.S. For 4 days now I haven't been getting any mail except from you.

▧ Because Dr. G. authorized a visit, Marilyn could be taken to her friends' room in a wheelchair—no sneaking around anymore.

MONDAY [MAY 1]

Well, here is more news about Irene! She was taken by ambulance to University hospital in Mpls Saturday morning to be treated there. I wrote her a letter this morning and I think she'd appreciate hearing from you folks, too. It's so foggy today and oh, so lonesome all alone again. Everyone kids me about being mean to my roommates! Ha! They all liked Irene so much too. Don't know if she'll be back here or not. Hope so.

MONDAY NOON [MAY 1]

I got your wonderful box this morning and say, Keith, thanks so much for the very cute May basket. Also Grams & Nita for the cookies, etc. Got a nice letter from Dottie Johnson this morning & she sure is a <u>real friend</u>! Nothing much has happened and I haven't heard from Irene. Am going down for an aspiration again this afternoon. It's been 4 weeks since I was aspirated. When we were weighed, I gained 2 lbs so now weigh 100 lbs.

SATURDAY NOON [MAY 6]

Have just eaten dinner and I <u>can't</u> say much about it. Some kind of ground liver for meat! Ugh! Got all your many cards this morning after I got back from having my shampoo. Evelyn sure got it nice and clean and I went on a cart. Don't be alarmed. She forgot I went in a wheelchair so I got on the cart since she had it made up. It was so easy to just lie there and it didn't tire me out. Got a letter from Nadine this morning and she told about Prom 'n stuff. Also sent a dollar. Am feeling swell but oh so lonesome for company.

MON. MORN. [MAY 8]

I surely hope I can have my exam this morning. If & when I do, I'm going to try to stop in to see Martha Schrodt. Haven't seen her since she was on

C II. *Say, if you happen to think of it sometime when downtown would you get me a new tooth brush? Mine is going to pieces. I like the stiffest kind. Yesterday afternoon, Ruth Jones, a little white-haired old lady, stopped in for a while. She is the one I pointed out to Daddy when he wheeled me over to the reception room on Easter. She's only 4 ft 11 in tall and half Irish & half Jew and I guess she used to be an acrobat in a circus. Real jolly person. I'm so disgusted! I haven't heard from <u>any</u> of my aunts & uncles for over a month now. Except Nita. I've written them all, too.*

MONDAY NOON [MAY 8]
I just came back from my exam, and I did find out a few things. She said my blood is practically normal now, and it was quite low in hemoglobin when I first came in. I found out about the sputum tests that were taken – 3 of them. The first was negative, 2nd was positive, and 3rd was negative. That stuff acts so funny. You see, each was taken on a different day. But she said it was better. My fluid is forming very slowly now and she said she can't tell for sure but she thought it would go away completely before long. I asked her about taking lessons, and she said I'd better wait till next fall at the start of the new term because your credit counts on the state exam at the end of the year and, "Maybe," I said, "<u>then</u> I could take two subjects." All she said to that was – "Well, we'll see how things go along." My temp has been staying about the same & the highest it goes is 99 so she acted like that was good, too. Asked her what she thought about that new girl, Marion Swaser, as a roommate for me. Dr. Gorenflo said, "Yes, I've been thinking that and she seems like a nice girl. We'll see." (as usual, ha!) So now I am happy. Tra la, tra la! Gee, I hope Marion can be with me. Geepers, I'm so happy! I was just griping about not hearing from my relatives and what happens? I get a swell long letter from both Auntie Ruth & Uncle Mory & Peggy. Oh, honestly, they are just rare!! I laughed til the tears came. You folks really don't know what a "morale-lifter" letters can be. Don't you think this is about the most cheerful letter I've written yet?

TUESDAY [MAY 9]

Yippee! I have a new roommate! Yes, this morning, Mrs. Swenson moved Marion Swaser from Little Falls in with me & is she ever nice. She is more on the quiet type and we are going to rest a lot because she is still running a little temp. Gee, were those flowers ever beautiful. I'm going to give some of them to different people on the floor! They stayed so nice, too, but when I opened the box a whole pile of dirt fell out in my bed. What fun cleaning it out! Mr. Waddell was up and brought me a beautiful amaryllis lily.

SATURDAY [MAY 13]

I am ashamed of myself for not writing the last few days, but maybe this letter will make up for it, huh? Wednesday I was aspirated and since then I've been running a little temp, and have been quite sore. My temp hasn't been 100 yet so I'm not worrying. Marion & I have been such sleepyheads. I guess everyone must think that's all we do, and it is, too. Thursday Marion's sister Agnes, from Minneapolis, came to visit her and went home on the 1:24 p.m. bus yesterday. She brought her a pile of magazines and sweets. Marion and I get along so swell. Gee, I like her. She's a very good cure-taker, too. She has sort of a reddish tint to her dark blond hair and big brown eyes. She is Catholic but that doesn't matter so much just so she is nice. Just now Mr. Waddell came in and gave Marion & I carnations for Mother's Day. Wasn't that nice of him? Marion got a white one as her mother is dead. Both her mother and father died here at the San & she & her sister & brother were here before 1938.

■ Marion's mother and father both died at Ah-gwah-ching— Stella in 1933 and Xavier in 1937—leaving four teenaged children: Aloise, Agnes, Florence, and Marion. Tuberculosis is not a hereditary disease, but it is easily spread among family members because of physical proximity.

MONDAY MORN [MAY 15]

I'm feeling okay now and my temp is down to normal again. Mrs. Swenson, our charge, just left yesterday until after she has the baby, so Miss Rothnem

is our charge, and Miss Sutter is again on our floor. Erna Hahn from La-
fayette is going to have 3 stages of rib surgery around the 25th or 26th of
this month. She has been over to see me quite a few times lately to get The
Herald and such. Her trouble is all cured, but her air space from fluid and
oil won't close without surgery.

▓ Lafayette is a small town northwest of St. Peter. Erna's first pneumotherapy treatments with air were not successful, so the doctor
performed an oleothorax, injecting either mineral or olive oil in
the pleural space. Erna's surgery, an extrapleural thoracoplasty,
would remove ribs on the same side as her diseased lung. The purpose was to make the lung permanently collapse, close the cavities,
neutralize the sputum, and stimulate the formation of scar tissue.
First done in Minnesota at the Mayo Clinic in 1919, it was a common tuberculosis intervention by 1945.

WED. MORN. [MAY 17]
Got your swell letter yesterday along with Nita's card & a card from Aun-
tie Ruth. I sure would have liked to be at the concert Sun. Gee, it seems so
funny not to see my name in the flute section! I'm feeling a lot better now
& Marion's temp is lower, too. Last night I put up my hair on the sides &
front and Evelyn parted & braided it for me. So now I'm going to have pig-
tails for the hot weather. My hair is really getting long. It was real hot here
yesterday so I had the window right next to me open and the little squirrels
came up so cute to peek in the screen. It's a regular nature study to watch
them so close up.

▓ In high school, Marilyn was in a flute trio with two other girls,
Mary Kneip and Ruth Ann Ritt.

FRIDAY AFTERNOON [MAY 19]
For the first time since I've been here we didn't have fish for Friday dinner.
Instead we had fried eggs and baked potatoes. Also scalloped corn, beet
pickles, Gram's coffeecake (yum, yum) tea, milk, and some luscious apple

Marilyn (left) in the flute trio at high school

pie. *All my mail comes in big bunches at one time. Boy what a haul I got this morning. I was so happy!*

■ Marilyn's "haul" did not go unnoticed. The next issue of *The Moccasin* asked, "By the way, Marilyn, how do you go about it? To rate ten letters at one delivery—we are very much interested."

* * *

Anne Marie sent a lot of books and programs from the different doings, all autographed by the kids for me. Different kids wrote little notes under their names saying they'd write soon, etc. Gosh, I could just sit for hours and look at it. It surely brings back the good old memories. There was also a nice letter from Nadine giving complete details on the Prom which I was waiting for so anxiously. She went with Vincent Anderson. You know, he's real nice and a good kid, too, but she said so many kids got drunk. I think it's really pitiful. We plan to have another popcorn party next week about

Thurs or Fri. I'm going to get permission from Miss Rothnem, and they will get passes so it's all lawful & legal. Ha! You'll never guess what "Oscar" did the other day! (Oscar is a she!) Well, she carried her two little baby squirrels around the corner of the B Building to a new nest in her mouth just like a cat carries her kittens. Honestly it was too cute for words!! And this morning the nurses were running around like wild trying to get a look at some new birds that have just come. They are two different kinds of orioles I think. Anyway, one variety is bright orange & red and the other is a lemon yellow—both with black markings. I've never seen so many beautiful birds in my life.

■ The abundance and variety of the avian population prompted Dr. Burns to initiate a bird banding project in 1932. The sanatorium received a permit from the Department of Agriculture to "capture migratory birds for scientific banding purposes." Recording the sightings gave patients something to do, and information on local birds' migratory habits was compiled and submitted. The program had been discontinued by Marilyn's time, but the bird population still entertained the patients.

* * *

P.S. Irene came back last night. Was I surprised.

P.S. Mr. Snyder is going home on the bus today for good. I'll sure miss him.

MONDAY [MAY 22]
Marion & I just had our baths and so we're all "fresh as a daisy" on this beautiful sunny morning. Haven't seen Irene yet, but have yelled back & forth to her through the hall & have written notes. She said she missed my torso under the covers in the other empty bed. She is still the same cheerful Irene with her jolly laugh.

TUESDAY [MAY 23]
♪ Oh what a beautiful morning. Up here it surely takes a long time for spring to come but when it does it sure is worth it!

8. FIRST SUMMER AT THE SAN

Gee, whiz, the days go fast

SAT. MORN. [MAY 27]

Well, today is Poppy Day and I suppose you'll be selling them early this morning. I bought one too and am going to put it on as soon as I get cleaned up for the morning.

■ Because of the poem "In Flanders Field," the red poppy came to symbolize the blood shed during World War I battles. In 1924, the distribution of poppies on Memorial Day became an official program of the American Legion.

* * *

John O'Donnell, the Ching "pin up" boy was over to see us last night and did we ever have a good laugh.

■ John O'Donnell was an older patient on the mend from tuberculosis. One of his duties as an "up" patient was to deliver mail to bed patients' rooms. He also made the rounds every evening as the self-appointed courier of love notes between the male and female floors. Marilyn described him as bald with yellowed skin. John had a breathing problem that made him hum and breathe at the same time, so she could hear him coming down the hall. His engaging personality was at odds with his appearance. He flirted with girls and entertained fellow patients with gossip.

WED. MORN. [MAY 31]

Gee, whiz, the days go fast. It hardly seems possible that school is out and Memorial Day past. I was thinking of you yesterday about 10 o'clock and thinking "Now the folks are starting out to the cemetery." We had sort of a holiday entertainment yesterday, too. The prisoners that work here at the San played a baseball game on the lawn over in front of the D Building so I got to see it.

■ Twenty-five prisoners from the St. Cloud Prison who were deemed to be low risk for escaping spent their summers at Ah-gwah-ching, helping with the dairy barn, harvesting, and grounds keeping.

WEDNESDAY EVE., MAY 31, 1944

This morning I after I read your letter I started asking different nurses and Dr. Callahan about resorts. They all seemed to favor "Paradise Point" which is owned by Mr. & Mrs. Golberg who work here. Mrs. Golberg is a nurse on our floor just now & she is so very nice, I'm sure you'll all like her. She said the cabins would be $10 a week, and they have one double bed in them but also could move in a cot. They have a stove and everything if you want to cook; otherwise Runyans is just a short ways from there. The place is a mile from here and sort of on a point so there is lake on two sides. They don't have electricity because the war prevented the line going out that far, but it is light so late now I don't think you'd mind using gas lamps. Mrs. Golberg said you wouldn't have to make reservations because there aren't many tourists now. Tonite Marion and I had quite some excitement. I was putting a cookie out for Oscar and what does he do but scoot right inside and on to my bed. Then he made for the floor down my bedpost and over under Marion's bed. Luckily the door was closed and so no one knew about it except us but I think everyone must have heard me yelling "Here, Oscar!" Gosh, but we were scared. He just wouldn't come back up to the window to get out again and we were so scared a nurse would walk in and he'd just as likely run out into the hall. Well finally, to end my talk, he jumped up on the radiator onto the window sill when I coaxed him with a cookie and I shoved him out. Whew! Was I relieved! They sure are tame little rascals. I was aspirated today and I just about fainted when Miss St. John told me how many cc's. Only 75 cc's for 2 weeks. That's pretty good considering I used to have 400 to 500 cc's.

SATURDAY [JUNE 3]

The last few days I've been taking it so easy because I'm quite sore from aspiration.

JUNE 7, 1944 [WEDNESDAY]

Well, Happy Birthday Keith! 12 years old! Boy, just think next year you'll be in Junior High & will be in your <u>teens</u>. Time sure flies. We got two more patients in last night. So we're filled up again. But I hear they are going to stop entering any new patients soon because they haven't enough help.

⬛ The sanatorium's report for 1943–44 noted an almost 100 percent turnover in personnel, particularly in nursing and dietary. In the July 1944 *Moccasin,* the editor listed new employees but said, "The employees come and go too fast for me to keep up." The employment of nurses at Ah-gwah-ching was always an issue, even before the war. In 1937, nursing turnover was 75 percent. Ah-gwah-ching's staffing problems were related to its location, isolation, and housing conditions. One annual report noted, "The isolation of the institution, the fact that tuberculosis is treated, and the lack of pleasant and homelike environment all tend to discourage employees for remaining for any considerable length of time." The sanatorium recruited nurses in the Twin Cities and nationally, with inducements such as hiring bonuses and train tickets to Walker. Some employees left before their probationary period was over.

* * *

Yesterday I sent to Sears for something. I'm not going to tell you what it is – want to surprise you. Anyway it's something to wear & only cost 59¢. I think it's fun to buy stuff by mail. I suppose you folks were all excited yesterday by the invasion news. Miss Sweeny, the nite nurse, told us about it at 6 o'clock in the morning when she came in with wash water so Marion & I listened in right away and kept our earphones on for 3 hours straight & different times during the day.

⬛ Because of the radio system, the patients kept current with war news. The Battle of Normandy began on June 6, when American, British, and Canadian forces landed on five beaches on the coast of France. The program schedule for most stations switched to an all-news format before dawn and continued that way until 9 AM Central War Time. Regular programming was interrupted by news bulletins throughout the day.

FRIDAY [JUNE 9]

I've been doing practically nothing because I always get a little temp after being aspirated. There was only 50 cc's this time, but now she's working it out with some kind of solution that helps stop the fluid. Gran asked about my toe. Well, I guess it's a little better, but still quite limp. It doesn't get in my way while walking, tho, when I have shoes on.

▪ The irrigation solution to which Marilyn referred may have been sterile saline.

MONDAY MORNING, JUNE 12, 1944

I'm feeling just fine today but Marion has had a little sick spell since last nite & isn't much better today. She sweats just terribly and has funny pains in her lung. Sometimes it's hard for her to breathe and she gasps for breath so it looks to me like she's developing fluid now, too. I sure hope not. I hope we are both feeling tops by next week when you come. Did you find the things I want to wear this summer? I'll list them again in case you forgot. 1. Pinafore; 2. Rose pleated skirt Alice gave me; 3. Yellow shorts (just thought of this now. I'd like to wear them in bed when it's hot), 4. Were there some white sandals Alice gave me last fall? I'd like to see them, too.

▪ Alice was Marilyn's first cousin in Iowa, daughter of Uncle Leon Barnes. She was older and had beautiful clothes, which Marilyn was happy to receive. In those days of scarcity, hand-me-down clothing was welcome.

WEDNESDAY MORNING [JUNE 14]

I know you all will be shocked as I was when I heard this news. My room-

mate, Marion, passed away yesterday morning at 1 o'clock. Day before yesterday, right after I wrote you, she wasn't feeling so good, the doctor moved her to a single room on BII and they called for her sister & brother to come from Minneapolis. It is so sad but she isn't suffering anymore which is a blessing. She was such a good girl – I'm sure Jesus has taken her to his Heavenly home. I'm all alone again, but I don't mind it so much as you are coming next week.

FRIDAY [JUNE 16]
Wednesday I wasn't aspirated so I suppose I will be next week. Ugh! I asked the doctor yesterday if I could move to BII porch, and she said she'd let me know. I am so disgusted with the roommate situation and I know I'd be ten times happier there. However, I'm not planning to move 'til after your visit because we can be alone in my room here.

■ Marilyn's family came to visit for a week. Keith, age twelve, was not allowed to come to her room because of minimum age

requirements for visitors. As Marilyn and her parents were sitting in her room, she looked out the window and said, "Dad, that looks like your car." A road went around the

**Marilyn, outdoors
for the first time in
nine months, with her
mother, Virginia**

lawn and up to the chapel, where there was a turnaround to come back to the building. And Keith was driving the car around because their father had left the keys behind. Their mother "went through the roof" and their dad ran out of the building right away to stop Keith. Marilyn's parents took her out in a wheelchair, her first trip outside since arriving in October. She remembered it was amazing to look up and see the sky. She and her mother posed in an Adirondack chair, a popular place for patients to have photos taken.

Marilyn's new roommate arrived after her family's visit. Valborg Storlie came from a farm near Mabel, in Fillmore County. The "Who's New" column in *The Moccasin* told readers that Valborg "has spent the biggest share of her life on the farm and can truly say she loves it. Besides the regular routine of housework she also spent much of her time gardening and raising chickens. The work at home, to be certain, has been left in good hands with her three young daughters (20, 17, and 15 years old) taking over during her absence." Valborg was fifty-one; once again, Marilyn had a roommate much older than herself.

WEDNESDAY [JUNE 28]

Brrr! Is it ever cold! I'm sure glad you came last week because it really was grand weather. Last night the wind was howling around the corners just like in winter. Carmie S. was over again last nite and showed Mrs. Storlie some pot holders she wants to buy. Olga was down, too, and Carmie said that some night she'll make some good coffee and bring it over to CII & us four will have a coffee party.

■ Carmen Seebeck was a tiny woman with a squeaky high voice and a southern accent whom Marilyn described as the most delightful fun. *The Moccasin* reported that Carmie Hunter was born in 1900 and lived in Kentucky until she was eighteen, when she married Ben Seebeck. She spent two years in the tuberculosis pavilion at Ancker Hospital in St. Paul and then transferred to Ah-

Carmie Seebeck and Tiny Rusten

gwah-ching. She wore a girl's size twelve dress and had a memorable personality. Because the sanatorium allowed her to have a one-burner hot plate and a coffee pot, she would make coffee for everyone in Building B and then bring some over to the women in C also. Marilyn remembered her as a cheerful, positive influence on everybody. For fun, short Carmie posed for a photo with a tall patient, Norman Rusten, known as "Tiny."

THURSDAY [JUNE 29]
I'm feeling "tops" today in spite of aspiration. She took off 100 cc's. I've heard from so many people that they think I have such swell folks and that goes <u>double</u> for me!!

SATURDAY, JULY 1ST

The other day Merle [Meryl] Essling was up here to show us some of the things the patients are making to send to the State Fair. She sure is nice but I still haven't seen her face without a mask.

■ Meryl was about twenty years old and from Minnesota. She interned in the occupational therapy department as a student from Ohio State University. From Ah-gwah-ching she went to spend six weeks at the Mayo Clinic and then an army hospital for six months. Because staff were required to wear masks, Marilyn became accustomed to recognizing people by their eyes. She imagined what their faces looked like, and then, if she saw them without a mask, she was surprised when reality didn't match her visualization.

* * *

Irene had her exam, and she is going to the U again instead of Walker and will go sometime in the next 3 weeks. She has already gotten darling baby things (she was over to show me them night before last) so I thought it'd be nice if you folks would like to go together with me on a little gift.

It's a darling little jacket Mrs. Osborne is making. It's made of soft flannel and she's embroidered the tiniest pink & blue flowers on it and around the bottom & sleeves – feather stitching. Also pink ribbons and it's only $1.25. She really should get $1.50 for it. Would

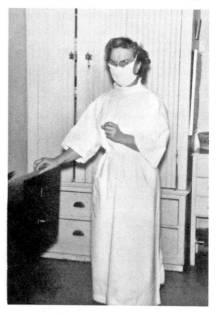

All employees wore masks when interacting with patients

you like to send me a little dough as I've been using up that you gave me so fast. Aren't I terrible?

JULY 3RD

Olga brought down the cute little baby jacket so I paid her for it last nite. I decided on a different one now and it's peach colored flannel with blue lambs & ribbons and flowers. Irene said she's planning on a girl and if it is her name will be "Mary Dee." Cute, eh? Nadine wrote me and she liked the Indian doll real well. Called him "Big Chief No-Can-Sit."

    ■ Olga delivered the jacket because Mrs. Osborne was on bed rest. Marilyn's gift to her friend Nadine was one of the dolls made by Native Americans at the sanatorium. Its legs didn't bend.

    * * *

Clara Kowalke had her company yesterday and looked so happy when she went by. She hadn't seen them for a long time.

    ■ Clara Kowalke, from Carver County, had been at Ah-gwah-ching more than four years, long enough for visitors to become infrequent.

    * * *

Today the nurses changed and we have Mrs. Munnell, that Indian nurse you thought was so nice that was on our floor last month, too, when you were here.

SATURDAY [JULY 8]

I sure hope I can move the first of August. I'm so fed up with this floor, and I just long to be with some younger kids. Irene told me she thot the change would do me good & Olga too but they said they'd all hate to see me go. And I sure would miss them too. Olga comes down every nite and we have such a good laugh.

    ■ Mrs. Storlie, though a pleasant person, was described by Marilyn as rather straitlaced, without much education or sense of humor. Aside from some handicraft work, they had little to talk about.

9: ROMANCE

I have reasons to be happy

MONDAY – JULY 10, 1944

I can't remember if I told you this but that day when I was outside with you I happened to look up at the C Building and noticed a boy on CIII looking at me with field glasses. Well, I asked John to find out who he was and he did. Boy—John's second name is "Cupid." This boy is 19 or 20 yrs old. Maurice Bensen "Benny" and he asked John all about me. John said I may get a letter from him any day now or he'll come down to visit me on Saturday. Woo! Woo!

▨ Marilyn's July 10 letter was to Keith, who was with their father at Camp Patterson on Lake Washington. The camp, founded in 1927 by the Mankato Downtown Kiwanis Club, still exists today. Marilyn told him about the squirrel's latest escapade.

* * *

Oscar came in on my bed yesterday and quick as a wink he found my bag of peanuts. That little rascal couldn't wait to get outside so he started burying the nuts under my blankets. We laughed so to see him pat the covers down over the nut with his little paws.

WEDNESDAY, JULY 12, 1944

Got your cards and I really was showered with mail yesterday. I have so many letters to answer now. Maurice Benson wrote me a letter last night and sent it down with John O'Donnell. He's coming down Saturday night to visit me. Oh boy! Woo! Woo! Mary Lou Kneeland & her mother dropped in on me Monday afternoon and were here 2 hours. They were so nice and brought me a box of Toll House cookies.

■ Mary Louise Kneeland was one year older than Marilyn and was the high school homecoming queen. She contracted polio after graduation and died in 1948.

* * *

I'm so sick of this floor. Honestly, if you think this floor is run good you're goofy. Things aren't what they used to be when Reece was here. And Miss Johnson, the cook, is so negligent. Honestly, this morning she gave me cocoa that was just curdled sour. Ugh! I just about threw up! Well, enough of this gripe. I'm feeling good, and I don't think I'll get sick after aspiration today.

FRIDAY, JULY 14 [FRIDAY AM]
Am having my hair shampooed this morn so I look nice for Sat. eve. Ahem! John brought me another letter from "him" last night. Woo! Woo! Asked Dr. G. if I could visit Florence N. & she said, "no." Would rather have F. come down here instead of me going up there. So that's settled.

JULY 14, 1944 [FRIDAY PM]
Golly, I got 2 letters from Benny today. Poor John! We really run him ragged! He came down tonite and asked me, "What's the idea of the double header?" Ha! Benny said in his letter tonite that he's coming down tomorrow nite. Oh boy! I got my hair shampooed and fixed real purdy so will "dazzle" him tomorrow. Also painted my long----claws! On his stationery I noticed his initials are Maurice J. Benson – M.J.B. – same as mine. Can you beat that? Isn't that a coincidence?

WED MORN [JULY 19]
Mabel was over yesterday afternoon and we had a nice visit. She didn't giggle so much. She had her year exam, but didn't get a privilege yet. She is negative now so was so happy over that. Mrs. Storlie and I are going to try

and finish our kittens today. Suppose I will be aspirated again but I don't mind that any more. I feel swell today.

    ■ The kittens were made of four-ply yarn wrapped around a simple rectangular cardboard frame. The roommates would tie off the yarn and then, with a razor, cut the yarn along one side and fluff it out to make a pom-pom. Each kitten needed one large pom-pom for the body and one small one for the head. Carmie had taught Marilyn how to make them, and now she had orders from several people.

[GAP IN LETTERS]

FRIDAY [JULY 28]

Dorothy Reetz was over last night and brought her crocheting along. Dorothy is such a "card." Gee, whenever we want a good laugh, we just invite her over. Got a letter from Benny last night. ♥ ♥ He said he wasn't feeling so good this last week but was better now. His folks and his only brother home on furlough are coming Sun. for a visit. All of my stationery is gone now so I just write on tablets. Do you suppose you could get some of that nice <u>name-on</u> stationery from Uncle Leon for me? If you could, I'd like it in some color (blue or pink) no white. Also with "Lynn" on it or my name and "Ching" address.

    ■ Uncle Leon owned newspaper offices and could have letterhead custom printed for Marilyn.

[LETTERS FROM AUGUST 2–3 MISSING; MARILYN HAD THE ENVELOPES]

MONDAY [UNDATED, PROBABLY AUGUST 7]

Yesterday Mrs. Storlie's sister-in-law and her husband came all the way from Fargo N.Dak. to see her. They were very nice people and brought her plums, peaches, cherries and grapes so we've been eating fruit galore. If you ever see any peaches would you send me a few some time. I'm just crazy for 'em lately. I seem to be getting a better appetite all the time. Yesterday we had steak, "stippen bread" and ice cream.

Stippen is a German word meaning "dipped." Stippen bread is dunked in steak juice, like the French au jus.

THURSDAY [AUGUST 10]

Well, I had my exam yesterday morning just after I mailed your letter. I didn't get a privilege but I'm on the list to go to the dentist now. Also my last sputum test was negative. Isn't that swell? Was aspirated yesterday and don't think it was very much. Last Wed. it was 40 cc's. It's been so terrible hot these last few days. And this morning it's already baking so we can expect to be "well done" by this afternoon.

▨ Without air conditioning or fans to cool them, patients suffered through the summer heat.

* * *

Mrs. Storlie and I are eating <u>so good.</u> Got all my stuff off for the fair and Miss Emig took my vanity set too so now I'll get $10.45 for all my stuff.

▨ In addition to showing craft items at the county and state fairs, sanatoriums also set up booths for selling. Marilyn's items possibly went to the Cass County fair in Pine River.

MONDAY MORN. [AUGUST 11]

It rained last nite so is real nice & cool this morning. For the last few days it's been real hot so I've been getting some use out of my shorts outfits. Yesterday when I was down for aspiration they had two fans going in the pneumo room so it was really comfortable. I didn't ask how much fluid I had but last week it was only 50 cc's. John was down and told me M.J.B. had surgery Wednesday so I've been writing him quite often. It wasn't very serious as they didn't have Kinsella & he wrote me a short (but sweet) note last nite. Everyone is just fine on our floor now <u>including</u> me.

SATURDAY, AUGUST 12, 1944

It got so cold last night we had our covers on. Today I'm feeling pretty good although not so well as usual. I have news for you, Mom. My dear little "cousin"

*from the Red River Valley came to visit me at last yesterday. So guess that's
a pretty good sign I'm getting better. Seem almost like old times again. Ha!*

▨ The cryptic wording is Marilyn's way of telling her mother that
she is menstruating again. Her monthly flow had been absent since
her health crisis in January; its appearance supported her opinion
that she was getting better.

* * *

*Mrs. Storlie & I have been just laying around all week. Just writing, sleep-
ing, & getting _fat_! Florence Novak wrote me the other night and was saying that Lucille Roiger is very sick & they don't expect her to last long. Her
fiancée is expected home on furlough from Italy so hope she lives until then.
Miss Willsie got me some real nice peaches in Walker. Only 26¢ for ½ doz.
P.S. Carmie just came over and said that Lucille Roiger died last nite.*

MONDAY MORN. [AUGUST 14]

*Carmie was over and she feels so bad about Lucille. I went in on the fund
for flowers. We didn't do much yesterday (Sun.) & just listened to the radio, read the paper, and I started a new book.*

*Have you heard from Uncle Leon about the stationery? I need it
pretty bad.*

WEDNESDAY [AUGUST 16]

*I'll be aspirated and may go down to the dentist if I'm called. Yesterday I
finished my sleeve on the sweater and today plan to work on the other. I
have a little more ambition these nice cool days. Guess what Miss Sutter
brought me yesterday? A big blue hydrangea that she had transplanted
from my Easter plant in her garden. It's just beautiful and I have it in with
a bouquet of glads Mr. Waddell brought over.*

FRIDAY MORN. AUGUST 18, 1944

*Well, I bet you're surprised in getting all these letters from me. Miss Will-
sie is giving me a shampoo this morning, and I've got a little toothache.
Haven't had that dratted tooth pulled yet.*

John was down last night as usual and he didn't bring any letter from Benny. He wasn't sick either because John said he was playing cards when he stopped in. Oh well, I probably will get a letter from him this morning in the mail.

▦ Marilyn also asked her father to build some frames for making her craftwork kittens. She used cardboard but wanted more durable ones made of Masonite. She asked him to make three pair so she could give sets to Mrs. Storlie and Carmie.

MONDAY A.M. [AUGUST 21]

The time sure flies. I think it's gone the fastest since Mrs. Storlie has been my roommate. We get along good and have the best time. Everyone thinks she's a pretty good mother for me. So you won't have to worry about anything with "Ma" Storlie and "Pa" O'Donnell to look after me. Ha! There was quite a bit of company here but before long I'll be one of the lucky ones having company, too. Do you know about when you'll be coming? I hope you don't come on a Wednesday or Thursday because you know I'm aspirated <u>every</u> *week. I'm feeling just swell as usual.*

TUESDAY [AUGUST 22]

Guess what we had for breakfast? Muskmelon and fresh apricot jam for our toast. Mmm! Yesterday we had our first sweet corn, so that really was a treat. This last week we've had exceptionally good meals. Last night Olga was over and she was sitting on my bed talking but who should whiz by in a wheelchair but Irene Lahti. We both yelled, "Hi!" but the nurse didn't stop. She's going to have a private room because she is negative and they don't want her to be with positive patients.

▦ Irene Lahti gave birth to the girl she hoped for but returned to the sanatorium to continue her treatment.

* * *

Say, Daddy, thanks ever so much for making those swell frames. I gave Mrs. Storlie a pair and also Carmie. They both say "Thank you" too.

WEDNESDAY MORN [AUGUST 23]

Well, last night I finished my last kitten for the Fair and I wish you could see it. It's French beige – sort of a reddish brown and has green eyes, green ribbon, and a ball between its paws. Now that I have everything done, I'm going to take a rest from fancywork and just read & write and maybe draw if I feel like it.

■ At the Minnesota State Fair, all of the state's sanatorium entries were in Class 225, "Work by the Physically Handicapped." They were listed by town location, not the name of the sanatorium.

* * *

One of my back teeth has been aching something awful lately and last night a piece of the filling & tooth broke off so am going to ask Gorenflo if I can go down to the dentist this morning. I wouldn't be surprised if he pulled it. If I have my exam this morning I'll ask the doctor then.

■ The patients were expected to brush their teeth every morning, using an emesis basin specifically for that purpose. Even though there was a dentist on staff, Marilyn had not had her teeth examined since her admission.

* * *

We have Miss Willsie again for personal nurse. Gee, I'm so glad. We were so afraid we'd get one of those dumb Indians.

■ Marilyn praised the Native girls who trained as nurse's aides. She described them as nice, jolly, and fun, and they gave her a good impression of Native Americans. However, with the exception of Mrs. White and Mrs. Munnell, who had been her personal nurses, most of the other Native nurses did not gain favor with her.

* * *

Benny is getting along just swell now, I guess. He said he sure picked one heck of a time to get sick. He has 17 orders for billfolds to make and by the time he's well enough, the orders will probably be cancelled.

■ The occupational therapy department had difficulties finding supplies because of war shortages—except for leather. Leather was scarce on the open market, but occupational therapy departments had priority for ordering it. Patients at Ah-gwah-ching sold billfolds at a store in Walker and received orders from all over the United States.

* * *

Agatha wrote me yesterday and I was so shocked to hear that Francis (Ben) Thieman was killed in action. He was in high school with me and we always got such a laugh out of him.

▓ Francis Thieman, in the US Marine Corps, died on July 2, 1944, just twenty-one days short of his twentieth birthday.

AUGUST 24, 1944, THURSDAY

Hi ya folksies! This is Toothless Annie herself speaking to you from station O-U-C-H! Yep! That's right. I done gone and had me "toofie" pulled. Dr. Wayne performed the operation at 10:45 a.m. yesterday (Wed.) morning. I was aspirated and then sat right down in line for the dentist. He looked over my teeth and wrote down all the cavities etc. and then drilled out my old filling in the molar to see if he could save it. But it was too far gone. When it was out he showed it to me and there already was a little abscess started on the end of the root so am sure glad he pulled it instead of filling. It bled quite a little but I went to sleep in the afternoon, and it didn't hurt anymore. It's a little sore on my jaw today, but otherwise I'm feeling swell! They can't get me down that easy!

SAT. MORN. [AUGUST 26]

Just a line to let you know I'm feeling swell now. Last night I put up my hair as M.J.B. is coming down tonite. <u>Oh happy Day</u>!! I have to look purdy you know, & I'm going to put on my slacks and pink blouse. Yesterday Olga was over and all of us (Mrs. S, Olga and I) were working on kittens. John brought the afternoon packages up and I got one from Cousin Helen and Dorothea in St. Paul. It was two boxes of Fanny Farmer candy. Boy, is it yummy.

▓ Helen Borges was a cousin of Grandmother Laumann, making

her granddaughter, Dorothea Koch, Marilyn's third cousin. The strong relationships among Marilyn's small extended family provided important emotional support.

MONDAY MORN. [AUGUST 28]

Say, was I ever happy when I read on your card that you'll be here next Saturday! Yippee! Are you going to stay until Labor Day and who all is coming? Bennie was down Saturday nite for quite a long time so we had a swell visit.

WEDNESDAY [AUGUST 30]

Am sorry I didn't get a card off to you before this, but we were called down for aspiration before 9 o'clock and I had to get ready. Boy, did I ever have fun today. I was the only girl there with 4 boys! Yippee!! Was down there for over an hour and when I finally did get back everyone thought I'd been kidnapped. Ha! When I came "home" there on my table was a letter from Benny so I have reasons to be happy. Gee, I'm sorry about "Tippy." He was such a darling pup. I know you'll all miss him so. We seem to have the worst luck with dogs!

■ The family dog Tippy lived in a doghouse. He was frightened by a thunderstorm, ran away, and was run over. The Barnes later adopted another dog, also named Tippy, which became Keith's dog because Marilyn was away.

THURSDAY MORNING [AUGUST 31]

This will probably be the last card I'll write before I'll see you so had better get busy and tell you some of the things I want. We have only had sweet corn once this summer so wondered if you could bring some up. They cook it for us in the kitchen. Also if you are bringing any soft drinks, I'd like root beer or orange drink instead of ginger ale. Uncle Mory wrote yesterday another one of those picture letters. I get such a kick out of them.

■ Her family visited on Labor Day.

10. SECOND YEAR BEGINS

You know I like to laugh & have fun

THURSDAY MORNING [SEPTEMBER 7]

Guess what?? We on CII no longer have Dr. Gorenflo *for a doctor. Starting yesterday we have Dr. Crow. Crow has the C Building; Gorenflo– B Building; Dr. Johnson –D Building; Dr. Sanderson – E Building. I'm so happy. Everyone says Crow is the best doctor here. He is very good at special things like aspiration and pneumo, and yesterday morning he aspirated me. Now since the change, we go at 9 o'clock in the morning instead of afternoon. And oh, you should see the kids I talk to down there. They are some of the cutest boys from CIII and CIV and I'm the <u>only</u> girl that has fluid on CII. Yesterday I had quite a visit with Earl Bemis, one of Benny's pals from CIV and is he handsome! (swoon, swoon!) He's about 21 years old and got dark wavy hair, brown eyes and dimples. When Miss St. John introduced me to him, I said, "John has told me quite a bit about you," and he said, "John has told me quite a bit about <u>you</u>, too." Yi! I didn't know what to think. Mrs. Storlie & John are always saying they have to look out for me to be my chaperones. They say Dr. Crow is more lenient than Gorenflo. I mean lets you have a little more exercise when you are able. So I'm sure I'll get a bathroom privilege at least at my next exam. He is okay for aspiration . . . does it real fast & gets it over with. I sure was scared, though, before he aspirated me. My teeth were doing a boogie-woogie chatter.*

THURSDAY MORNING, SEPT. 14, 1944

Dr. Crow called me down for an aspiration real early in the morning and by the time I got back the mail had already gone out. He didn't hurt me at *all yesterday and I'm feeling just as good as ever. If anyone should happen to ask you what I want please tell them <u>no</u> candy or food or perfume or hankies. I like money (who doesn't) but most of all I'd like an identification bracelet to wear on my wrist. Oh, I'm just crazy about them and that's the only thing I can think of unless it would be a charm bracelet or friendship bracelet with the names of my friends on each link. I don't want much, eh? But you always ask me to write what I want so this time I really told you.*

▨ Marilyn did get a charm bracelet from her friends, for Christmas. It was sterling, with little hearts, and each heart had a friend's name engraved on it.

* * *

The other night I got 4 "locals." John sure came back from the B building with his pocket full.

▨ "Locals" were all the notes and letters written to another patient within Ah-gwah-ching. US Post Office rules dictated that any mail handled by a postal employee had to carry postage, even if mailed and delivered within the sanatorium, so patients saved on postage by using John's delivery services.

* * *

Benny is going to the show "Pin-up girl" today and Saturday will be down to see me if nothing happens in the meantime. He had oil put in his lung Tuesday & wasn't feeling so hot but is better now.

TUESDAY AFTERNOON [UNDATED, PROBABLY SEPTEMBER 19]
It's a real cloudy, rainy day so I'm in a good letter writing mood for home & besides have some news to tell you. Well, I might as well begin with that right now – you see, Mrs. Storlie hasn't been feeling so good for the past month or so (this "change of life" stuff) and is awfully nervous so she can't stand much noise. And she hasn't been eating as well or gaining any weight so she's asked the doctor if she could be alone in a room or with some other lady her own age. It isn't that we don't get along. We never quarrel over a thing, but you know I like to laugh & have fun & have kids over to the

room. Well, in that way we are as different as day & night. She's used to the farm where things are quiet and I like "lights, color, and action." She isn't the type that can meet & talk with people & I like people in general, so we've been talking it over and are now trying to work it out some way. She had her exam this morning so the doctor said he'll see about it. Well, it happens that Joan Shippey is all alone at the time, too, and she heard that Mrs. Storlie wants to move or be alone so Joan wrote me a note asking me to move in with her. She hates to be alone and is just about as well as me – we're both negative and more the same age, like to have fun, etc. So tomorrow I'm going to ask Crow if Joan and I can get together.

Later—

Rothnem just was here & they are going to move Mrs. Storlie in with Mrs. Larson down the line and maybe tomorrow I can move in with Joan. Well, anyway, tonight I'll be alone again. Ah, sweet solitary confinement! Well, here comes the moving van so I'll have to stop for now.

6 p.m. –

Well, here I go again. ♪ "I'll walk alone." ♪ Ta dum de dum! That ought to be my theme song, don't you think? Ha! Gee, I got a nice letter from Joan just now. She said she hoped she'd see my bed being moved into her room tomorrow morning. Gosh, there sure has been a big hullabaloo about this moving business. But then as Joan said, quoting Oscar Wilde, "There's only one thing worse than being talked about and that's <u>not</u> being talked about." Ha! Yesterday I got so much mail.

▌ Marilyn listed her letters. Some were from school friends, whom Marilyn said were so good to write, but all they talked about was football games, homecoming, and the Library Club initiation. She wanted to hear more news about them and their lives.

* * *

I've invited Carmie Seebeck, Lucille Larson, Olga, & Florence down for a little party of ice cream & cake on the afternoon of my birthday and they all can come. Miss Rothnem is arranging it so I can get the ice cream that afternoon. They'll send it out from Walker by bus.

▪ Throwing a birthday party was no easy task. Each of the women Marilyn invited had to have the right "privilege" in order to come and needed to ask a doctor for permission to leave the floor.

* * *

Say, Mom & Nita, please don't write anything personal about any patients here on your cards. Sally Jackson sorts all our mail before we get it & I wouldn't be surprised if she reads it. She and her mother are the two biggest gossips in the San. Olga calls them the "blue-bloods." They have to have the newest bedpans without necks, and their room mopped first in the morning, and the first tray meals, and well – everything first. One night when Olga was going back to her room she stopped and took a nice new white bed pan off the cart where they had been neatly stacked for the night routine. The nurse saw her & told her not to take it because it was for Sally and her mother. Olga just gave her a dirty look and said, "I don't see why their behinds are any better than mine." Gee, I sure laughed when she told me about it.

▪ The universal bedpans had urinal necks for male use, and Sally and her mother didn't want to use those.

THURSDAY, SEPT. 21, 1944 (1ST DAY OF FALL)
I had quite a talk with Bemis yesterday and did I ever blush! Ruby St. John wheeled him out from fluoroscope and asked him where he wanted to be and he said over on the other side of the hall (That's where I was.) Dr. Crow was standing in the doorway and St. John said to him, "I think there's more than one boy down here that's glad you took over CII!"

SEPT. 25, 1944 [MONDAY]
Dear Keith,
We just finished our breakfast and it's 7:30 so maybe you aren't even up yet. At different times of the day I like to sit and think of what all you folks are doing back home. When I used to do that I'd get <u>so</u> homesick but <u>them days is passed & gone forever</u>. I really am having a good time now up here &

Universal urinal/bedpan

it really seems like home. On Wednesday mornings when I go downstairs to be aspirated, I always talk about my room as being "home" and all the other patients do too. There sure must be a lot of "homes" here then, cuz there are over 400 patients. Olga, one of my friends on CII and I are going over to the Library next week and have some pictures taken. I hope they turn out good so you can all have a picture of me. On those ones taken outside I looked awfully skinny!

■ It was an Ah-gwah-ching tradition to have one's photograph taken while sitting in a particular chair in the library. The library area had been remodeled and was one of the nicer spots on campus.

* * *

Yesterday (Sunday) was very quiet and my roommate & I just read the Sunday paper & listened to the good radio programs.

■ Joan and Marilyn became roommates. Joan's husband, Virgil, had been a medical corpsman but was in a prisoner of war camp.

**Marilyn posing in the library,
an Ah-gwah-ching tradition**

She wrote a V-mail (short for Victory Mail, special delivery for the armed forces) letter to him almost every day. V-mail letter-sheets combined writing surface and envelope into one piece of paper. V-mail correspondence was reduced to thumbnail size on microfilm, and the film was sent to a receiving station near the addressee. The letter-sheets were reproduced about one-quarter their original size and delivered. This saved shipping space during the war because 150,000 one-page letters could be reduced to fit into one mail sack.

Joan's brother Donovan was in the Army Air Corps, her brother William was fighting on the western front, and her brother James was also a prisoner of war. Her five-year-old son, Joey, lived with her parents, the Oseths, in Alexandria, Minnesota.

* * *

My boyfriend, Benny, was down to see me again Saturday nite. And, oh, we had fun. He goes to the shows every once in a while now and is up more than me. I sure hope Dr. Crow gives me a privilege soon so I can be up too. I feel so darn good and am gaining weight like everything.

Love & Lipstick, your sister, Marilyn

p.s. I'm also sending along a letter to Mom that I got from Phyllis Tatge.

■ Phyllis, the editor of *The Moccasin*, was a patient on BIII, so she and Marilyn had few opportunities to see each other. She asked Marilyn to thank her mother for sending a magazine called *New Voices*. "Since you've been on the cure," Phyllis wrote, "you know how much the thoughtfulness of others helps us, so I think it very good of your mother. Do tell her for me."

[UNDATED PARTIAL LETTER, SOMETIME IN EARLY OCTOBER]
When Miss Lyford brought my text books last Monday I noticed they were the same as we had in school. Say, that reminds me – did you ever sell my last year's books? If you didn't I wish you would cuz I paid quite a bit for them.

■ Marilyn described her teacher, Florence Lyford, as tall, thin, and gray-haired. Miss Lyford brought books to Marilyn and gave assignments but was not helpful in explaining the material. Her mission seemed to be saving souls; she also gave Marilyn religious tracts and advised against listening to radio broadcasts of the Mormon Tabernacle Choir because that was "sinful music."

* * *

Also was wondering about my flute. Couldn't you send it in soon and have it sterilized etc. because I think you should sell it now while you can get a good price. Then you could put that money in my bank account. I have so many flute books & solos that I bought from Mary Kneip. If they could be lamped I'm sure one of the flutists would like to buy them. Please tell me all about these matters in your next letter. I have my first lesson this afternoon at 3 o'clock. Oh boy!

■ Items that were considered contaminated by tuberculosis bacteria could be sterilized by exposure to ultraviolet rays for about one hour—commonly by putting them under a carbon arc or alpine lamp.

WEDNESDAY AFTERNOON

[UNDATED, POSSIBLY OCTOBER 11, PAGES MISSING]

I was downstairs and was aspirated this morning and had fun <u>as usual</u>! Earl Bemis was there so we got to talk a lot with each other. That guy has <u>personality</u> – <u>plus</u>! When Andy, the orderly from CIV, took him back they waited for Willsie to bring me in the wheelchair so we'd get to ride up in the elevator together. When I got in the elevator along side of him he said, "Sure, now I'll get a chance to hold your hand." And he did, too! More fun – these San romances.

[UNDATED INCOMPLETE LETTER, POSSIBLY OCTOBER 18, PAGES MISSING]

We sure had fun down at aspiration yesterday morn. Gordy Greene, Glenn Haglund, Earl, Johnny Hanst, Pearson, & I were all down there and what a gab session! Mrs. Storlie is feeling so much better now & eating & sleeping so good. She's gained some weight, too, I believe. Was I surprised when John came down and told me this bit of news – Mr. Snyder from St. Peter is back at the San. He had some kind of an operation that took him down quite a bit.

SUNDAY NITE [UNDATED, PROBABLY OCTOBER 22]

It's been so sunny and nice. The trees are so beautiful but soon they'll be bare. I hate to think of winter – it seems so sad-like but I'm sure this winter will be a much happier one than last. Honestly folks, I've never seen such gorgeous scenery in fall as up here. Even the road along by the State Hospital [in St. Peter] *can't compare with this. When I was sitting on Joan's bed by the window, I could see the gorgeous red maple trees over the Seldom Inn and gosh, I got a homesick streak – not really but it reminded me of our maples out in front of the house and of so many things. The way we used to press them, the leaves, and how we used to go around at Halloween. You sure get to thinking of all the wonderful old times when you're up here. I never really miss all of it until I sit down and actually think about things. Guess I shouldn't do that but its sorta fun when you have so many good memories – and I surely have that!*

▦ The original cottages at the sanatorium had names like Seldom Inn, Rest-a-While, and Pine Grove.

* * *

Olga was over tonight and telling us all the gossip, etc., about roommate troubles and such. She said, "Boy, I hope when I get to Heaven I don't have to have a roommate." Gee, I got a kick out of that. Then, Norman Rusten, alias "Two-ton Tiny" (he weighs almost 300 lbs.) was in and showing us some little baby booties he crocheted. Of all things! A big lug like that and all he can find to do is sissy work!

▦ Norman Rusten later worked as a rural mail carrier out of Bemidji. His obituary noted his stay at Ah-gwah-ching and that while there he learned to crochet—a hobby he continued after he left.[5]

* * *

Now for some good juicy gossip. Guess what? (you never could.) Dr. Gorenflo is going to have a baby! And she was the career type of woman (I thought). She's probably in her early forties. Well, that just goes to show you what a war will do. Ha!

■ Dr. Gorenflo was married to E. Farrell Creech, a forester and supervisor of a Civilian Conservation Corps camp. Their son was born on April 9, 1945, and she was thirty-eight years old.

* * *

Benny was down to see me last night and he told me something that just about made me bawl. He's going to have surgery in 2 or 3 weeks and will go down to Mpls. to St. Mary's Hospital for it because they aren't having any more surgery up here. They don't have enough nurses. He's having what is called a lobectomy – a very serious operation where they remove one of the lobes of his lung. They say it's very dangerous because it takes so long – 6 to 8 hours and it's so easy to have internal bleeding. Oh, I hope & pray he'll come through it all right cuz he's a nice kid and so young. I'll miss seeing him but will write real often. He'll probably be there 2 months or more. I sure wish he could be back by Christmas.

■ Operations to remove parts of lungs had become more common by 1945 but still carried significant risk of complications from infection.

WED. MORN. 10 O'CLOCK [OCTOBER 25]
Dear Daddy, Keith, & Nita,
Mom and Grams arrived safely yesterday at about 5 o'clock & we had a swell visit last night. Gee, it's good to see them!

SUNDAY MORNING, OCT. 29, 1944
Benny came down last night & we had a good time. Lloyd Polo came down with him and oh, is that kid corny. He just kept us laughing all the time. Benny sat on my bed & Polo on the chair so I was quite the popular gal last night. Everyone that went by just stared. I guess they weren't used to seeing boys in my room.

11. HOLIDAYS 1944

Gee, but I feel wonderful these days!

SAT MORN. [NOVEMBER 4]

It's another cold morning. Brrr! I had on my snuggies under flannel pj's and 3 wool blankets last night. Nothing much happened since I wrote last. I'm feeling swell except for the visit from my "cousin." Want to get busy at my History, so 'bye.

MON. NIGHT [NOVEMBER 6]

It's almost rest hour but wanted to tell you the good news. I was weighed this afternoon and gained 5½ lbs. Isn't that super? I weigh 114 lbs now so by the 1st of Jan. I'll be 120 no doubt. Had my lesson this afternoon and it went okay but I sure hate History. Tomorrow's the big day! Oh boy, I wonder who'll win.

November 7, 1944, was Election Day. Incumbent Democrat Franklin D. Roosevelt defeated Republican Thomas E. Dewey.

* * *

Got your swell letter this morn, Mom. Thanks a lot. Here are the answers to your questions. No, I don't get tired during lessons. I do a little bit every morn & if I don't feel good, don't have to do it at all. It takes a year to get a credit if you pass the exams in the spring. I'm sure not going to overdo this Xmas. Really I haven't done any fancywork for weeks and am not going to until after Xmas I think.

SAT MORN [NOVEMBER 11]

Am feeling swell as usual and there really isn't much more news to tell.

Thursday I received a letter from Mary Lou Connor & several other girls in my class had written notes to me on it. I sure got a kick out of it. Wish they'd do that more often. Am going to listen to "gab session" with Clellan Card now so 'bye.

■ Marilyn referred to *Almanac of the Air*, a popular radio show on Minneapolis's WCCO radio that ran for eight years starting in 1936. Clellan Card is mostly remembered for his television show for children, *Axel and His Dog*, which aired on WCCO from 1954 to 1966.

NOVEMBER 16, 1944 [THURSDAY]

I'm feeling just swell today after aspiration and think I'll have a shampoo this morning. I sure do need one. We're both going to have a check-up on our eyes by Dr. Lee, the specialist who comes out here every 2 weeks. We still haven't gotten down to the dentist yet. He's so slow! Yesterday, he wasn't here at all – went deer hunting! I had my exam yesterday afternoon from Dr. Crow and had pretty good news. My temp is normal all the time now, my sputum tests have been negative since April, my sedimentation went down from 20 to 14 this time (that's just 2 points above normal), and my blood pressure is normal so that makes me pretty happy. He said my fluid is getting better and thinks it will clear up with the continuation of irrigation. But they are going to have to do something about collapsing my lung again and that pneumo I took last fall didn't help much I guess. You see, I have too many adhesions at the top of my lung & they can't be cut because they're too thick. So he said if I don't stay negative – that is negative culture – I'll have to have some kind of surgery. Either an "extrapleural" (that's where they remove part of a rib in order to make a space to give you pneumo) or maybe a few ribs out. I felt the tears coming to my eyes when he told me that but fought them back pretty well. And I'm so glad he told me because I wanted to know the truth instead of being led on like Gorenflo did to me.

■ Sedimentation is how fast the red blood cells settle, leaving clear serum above. While not a diagnostic tool, it can indicate chronic low-grade infection and perhaps the presence of a TB lesion. And tests taken in sequence can indicate improvement.

* * *

It makes me feel bad but there always is the chance my lung will heal without surgery as he said. And if it doesn't, surgery isn't the worst thing in the world and if it helps me – that's the main thing. I'm just going to keep my chin up and pray to God that everything will turn out for the best and I know you all will, too. Don't worry about this getting me down, now Mom, cuz I'm not going to let it and that's that! I'll show that old "bug" a thing or too yet.

P.S. Say, when Daddy comes up could you bring me some potato chips & a few candy bars (that is if you can find them).

MONDAY MORN [NOVEMBER 20]
It was such a nice day yesterday—really the 1st day of sunshine this month. I hope it is nice on Thursday when you're up here, Daddy. I s'pose you'll be coming on the 5 o'clock bus Wed. afternoon so as to be here all Thursday. Am I right? I wrote out (or rather, addressed) quite a good bunch of Xmas cards so now have about ¾ of them ready to go off. It sure is a lot easier this way. Had such a nice letter from Mrs. Goodell Saturday. She thinks Leonard will be in service by next June when he graduates. I want to send a Xmas card to Dean Myrum who's in the Navy. Could you please get his address for me? Miss Sutter will be giving us baths now, so Bye.

WEDNESDAY [NOVEMBER 22]
It's 7:30 right now so suppose Daddy is already on his way. Boy, I'll be so happy to see him! I was aspirated yesterday morning on account of Thanksgiving so I'm glad that's over with for another week. Heard from Ethel Nimps yesterday. She's a nurse's aide at Glen Lake.

THANKSGIVING MORN. [NOVEMBER 23]
Oh – is this ever a beautiful day! It snowed yesterday & everything is such a gorgeous white. Daddy got here last night at 5:30 and we're having a swell

visit. Right now he's reading my new "Life" magazine while I'm writing this. Don't know what we'll have for dinner but it's going to be good! I'll leave a space and write it in afterwards. Jeepers, thanks so much for all the wonderful things you sent up. This was almost a regular Christmas ahead of time.

▧ In the space left on the postcard Marilyn listed turkey, mashed potatoes and gravy, dressing, cranberry sauce, hot rolls, milk, teas, tomato on a lettuce leaf, celery, olives, and pumpkin pie with whipped cream.

SAT. MORN. [NOVEMBER 25]

Just a note before Miss Sutter comes in to fix us up. Am listening to a piano solo on Dayton's so please excuse me if this is all jumbled up.

▧ *Dayton's Musical Chimes* was a morning show on WCCO radio. Howard Viken would say "Good morning" and then "Here's your Dayton reporter." The reporter was Joyce Lamont, but her name was never mentioned. The program promoted records from Dayton's department store by playing snippets of songs, and then Lamont would talk about the song or the singer.[6]

* * *

Just wanted to tell you that just after Dad left yesterday, Joan's mother & in-laws came up to visit her. They are so nice & brought all kinds of stuff for us such as chicken sandwiches, Cokes, cake, pie, jelly & jam, etc. We didn't get tired though as we just layed around most of the time and slept so good last night. Benny is coming down tonight and also visit Bob Kaiser on BII. He had pneumonolysis (adhesions cut) yesterday.

MONDAY, 7:30 A.M. [UNDATED, PROBABLY NOVEMBER 27]

▧ This letter, labeled PRIVATE, contained Christmas gift secrets.

SAT. MORN [DECEMBER 2]

Heard Mr. Snyder is getting steadily worse. His temp was 103° yesterday morn. I don't think he'll last long now. Isn't that too bad? Joan got her first culture yesterday. Was she excited! She had wonderful news at her exam and is getting 1 bathroom privilege in a few days or so. Pretty swell, eh? Say, how about sending me some Xmas seals (T.B.)?

■ Patients in the wards earned "privileges" based on their progress to healing. On January 25, 1943, Dr. Callahan distributed an explanation of the privilege system:

One Privilege a Day:
May go to bathroom once a day.

Two Privileges a Day:
May go to bathroom once in the morning and once in the afternoon.
Take water glasses along in the afternoon.
Show [that is, movie] twice a month, in a wheel chair.
Keep bedside tables tidy.

Four Privileges a Day:
May go to bathroom as necessary. Fill own water glasses.
Tub bath or shower weekly.
Keep own lockers and bedside tables clean.
Show four times a month, and you may walk.

Visiting hours are from 5 to 6 p.m., only, and twice a week, for those having privileges.

Please do not over-step your visiting privileges, as it encourages others to visit who are strict bed.

Implementation depended on the charge nurses. Some were more rule-bound than others.

MONDAY [DECEMBER 11]
Lucille Niesen from BIII was down to see me Saturday night. She has full privileges now so can really get around. Then Erna Hahn was over last nite after church. She's up on full priv. too, so sure got along swell after her thoro. Just heard that Mrs. Soper will have surgery (thoro) in 2 weeks when Kinsella comes again.

TUESDAY [DECEMBER 12]

I sure feel swell—never seem to get tired. Guess that's cuz we take every rest hour. Mabel's birthday is Friday (15th) so I'm going to send her a cute card. Am giving Harriet 2 tiny bottles of perfume I got for a present one time (Honestly, I have so much perfume on hand. Hope I don't get any more for Xmas)

THURSDAY MORNING [DECEMBER 14]

Well, today I finish getting my Xmas cards off. Was down for aspiration yesterday and Dr. Crow said my fluid is <u>real</u> thin now so that means there isn't much pus in it anymore. Also my air space is almost closed and when that's completely closed, usually no more fluid forms. Oh boy – was I happy!

SAT. MORN [DECEMBER 16]

Here it is Saturday again. Hope somebody comes to visit. Was I surprised last night. I got a letter from Benny again. I sure have fun talking to Vivian Olson (Ole), a new nurse on our floor. She's from Walker and knows a lot of kids out here. She told me Bex said to her the other day, "That little blond on CII ain't bad." So now I'll have to watch out for that <u>wolf</u>!

■ Marilyn also reported that she received two more gifts in the mail and a subscription from the American Legion Auxiliary for *Charm* magazine. Her thank-you letter to the auxiliary was printed in the *St. Peter Herald*. The editor noted that the public heard so much about courage—courage of the fighting men, of war mothers, of war brides—but he thought the courage of those like Marilyn was something extra special.[7]

JANUARY 3, 1945

Quite a few things have been happening and are going to happen so thought I'd better give you all the dope. Well, they've started the moving – and how! Yesterday Vera Hanson moved in with Harriet (so that lets me out – I mean the chance of Joan & me separating). Really, it's a wonder the nurses can keep track of any of us. I hear the boys on CIII & CIV are having some

changes made, too. Bob Kaiser and Lloyd Polo are moving up to CIV as
they want to break up that "poker" gang. Benny will be going for surgery
and then Earl Bemis is probably moving down to CIII in his room. Bob
Kaiser, Polo, Hanson, and Ken Farley all sneaked down here last night "to
get their last look at women" so they said. They stopped in here for a while.
Golly, those guys have nerve! They were dressed in pajamas, bath robes and
slippers – and you know, I was just thinking how funny that would seem
to outsiders – boys coming down to see the girls like that. Course – we're in
pajamas too and think nothing of visitors seeing us like that. Mrs. Storlie
had her exam day before yesterday and guess what? Here she thought she
was negative and she's highly positive! And in two weeks she's going to have
a thoracoplasty. I was so shocked! Honestly, it makes a person lose faith in
doctors when they lead you on that way.

JANUARY 6, 1945
Mom, if they read my letter at the Legion meeting you heard that they're
starting penicillin treatments on me. Gee, I was so excited when Dr. Crow
told me last Wednesday. So many are taking it now & I guess it's working
swell. Gordy Greene and Bemis are taking it now and Kathy Wells and I
are starting next week. All of us are in the same boat – empyema! If I start
on Monday, I'll probably be going down every day to get punctured. More
fun! But I don't mind if it does the trick.

▓ Empyema is a condition in which pus gathers in the pleural
space between the lungs and the inner surface of the chest wall.
TB patients who had pneumothorax treatments were particularly
susceptible to developing empyema. Penicillin had been hailed as
a potential cure for tuberculosis, but tests in the 1930s showed that
it was ineffective. By 1943 the drug was being produced in large
quantities for use in the war zones, and many sanatoriums began
using it for TB-related bacterial infections. The mortality rate for
empyema at the time was estimated to be one in four, so receiving
penicillin injections was indeed good news.

* * *

We were weighed and I gained another 2 lbs. so now am 118. Didn't quite make the 120 like I wanted to but then –! Everyone that stops in can't get over how fat my face is. Gee, it makes me feel so good – you really don't know. And this morn Mrs. Abrahamson, our nurse, said when she was giving me a back rub "You certainly are getting <u>well padded</u>!" Benny, Ken Farley and Glenn Haglund were down here again night before last. They sneaked down in their bathrobes & slippers again for just a few minutes and then hurried back before old Weiber (alias the Stork) the night "snoopervisor" came flying by on her broomstick. Golly, I don't know what we'd do if we couldn't gripe about nurses & food around this place! Is it ever cold up in this here north country. It was 40° below yesterday morning and don't know what it is today. But I don't mind when I'm cozy & warm snuggled up in my Hudson Bay. Have gotten more compliments on that "pretty" blanket. Gee, but I feel wonderful these days! Have a wonderful temp, a wonderful appetite, and sleep just wonderful at night; in fact, too wonderful to stay on this <u>sick</u> floor. Yep! It's getting on me nerves again. Rothy sure irks me. We can hardly laugh any more or have company stop in to talk. "After all, you're here to get well." I've only heard that a thousand times. I know for a fact I couldn't have gotten along so well if I hadn't been happy. And I have to talk to people to be happy. It's just my nature I guess! They say half of the battle is your mental attitude and if you're happy.

▓ Nurse Rothnem performed several acts of kindness for Marilyn when she was more ill and quieter. Once Marilyn felt better, she had a livelier social life—a tonic for her emotionally but not beneficial physically. Nurses had seen many relapses, and Rothnem's strictness might have reflected concern rather than meanness.

* * *

Miss Emig was here Thursday and she's making plans for her art classes. She says she'd like to have me and first of all I'll have to study the fundamentals in drawing and then work up. And she'll teach me Fashion Designing as she taught that several years ago to some patients. She's really quite an artist – graduated from the Chicago Art Institute. I'm so excited.

12. SORROWS AND SHORTAGES

An awful lot of living to do when I get home

THURSDAY, JANUARY 11, 1945

Haven't heard from Benny yet so I'm hoping to get a letter in tonight's mail. John O'Donnell has been sick in bed with a cold all this week so he hasn't been down for a long time. The "love birds" around here sure miss him because there's no one else to deliver letters. Yesterday I had such a tiny amount of fluid – don't think it could possibly have been 50 cc's but I haven't started penicillin yet. He said not this week anyway because they have to start the worst cases before me.

[GAP IN LETTERS]

FEBRUARY 5, 1945

Will just dash a line off to you before we have baths as I wanted to tell you what happened. Yesterday (Sunday) afternoon at about 1 o'clock Dr. Crow called Joan down to his office to tell her they had received a telegram saying her brother, Don, was killed in a plane crash near Yuma, Arizona. He was the one expected home on a furlough this week. Miss Rothnem came back and told me after Joan was taken down there and I was so shocked. Joanie always spoke of him so much it seemed almost as if I knew him, too. He was 21 yrs old and a crew chief on a big bomber. She hasn't heard the details of the crash yet. Poor Joanie was just sobbing her heart out when they brought her back in the wheelchair and she cried all afternoon. She's taking it so hard because he was the only one of her brothers left in the States and they thought surely he was safe. Her brother Jim is a prisoner near Berlin

*so they were hoping he'd be home soon and her 19 year old brother, Bill, is
fighting on the western front and they haven't heard from him since that
German drive in December so don't know if he's safe or not. I guess she
feels the worst about her mother being all alone at home but her father is
coming in a few days from the coast. She wants to go home so bad and Dr.
Crow will let her know today if she can. They're going to have a conference
and decide from her x-ray. I do hope she can go because she'd feel so much
better about it.*

■ Marilyn later learned the details of the crash. There were four
men in the Flying Fortress and they were making a landing on the
Yuma, Arizona, field after their twenty-second mission or flight.
Just as they came down, a tractor of some sort was coming over
the hill, and the pilot thought it was another plane. He dipped a
wing, and they were so close to the ground that it hit and flipped
the plane. The plane spilled three hundred gallons of high-octane
gasoline, which exploded and burned everything.

FEBRUARY 12TH

*Mrs. Storlie is going to have her first stage of "the rib" a week from this
coming Thursday or Friday. Mrs. Soper is getting along okay from what
we hear but she was pretty sick the 1st 2 days. There are so many having
surgery now. Suppose I'll be the next one. Ha! John O'Donnell told me he
heard Benny was coming back this week. I wonder who told him and how
true it is. You know these sanatorium rumors!*

■ John O'Donnell's news about Benny's condition was not accu-
rate. In fact, Benny had already passed away on February 11 from
complications of surgery. For reasons unknown, that news was not
shared with Marilyn for a few days. There is a gap in her letters from
February 12 until almost a month later. Whatever details Marilyn
may have shared with her family in those letters are not known
to us, nor does she remember them clearly. Perhaps her mother
thought them too personal or heartrending to be saved. Marilyn

recalled that time, so soon after Joan's loss, as being very sad. She had known that the success of Benny's surgery was uncertain.

By 1945, after a year and a half residency, Marilyn was adept at adjusting to the realities of life and death at the sanatorium. Patients were braced for bad things to happen and, when they did, would come to terms with them. Day-to-day life was different from that in the outside world.

In early March, Marilyn received a letter from Ralph Kutz, who lived on CIII. They had met in the waiting line for treatment, and others had suggested to Marilyn that he would be a good friend for her.

SATURDAY [UNDATED, MARCH 3?]
Tomorrow (Sunday) nite I'm going visiting. Dr. Crow gave me permission to see Valborg as she is feeling fine now. She said she got your nice letter and appreciated it so much. Thanks so much for the crochet thread, peanuts & candy bars. I hope that's all I'll have to ask you for a while now. But we're so sorta helpless up here – and the nurses don't go into town very often.

■ If the nurses or any other employees who lived on campus wanted to go to Walker, they had to wait for the bus and pay fare, hitch a ride with the few who owned cars, or walk two and a half miles, which took about an hour each way.

* * *

I sure wasn't sleepy last night and didn't get to sleep til way after the night nurse came on at 11 o'clock. Maybe that's cuz I got another letter from Ralph last night. Ha! Gosh but he writes cute! He's 21 and his home town is Stillwater, but he was in the Merchant Marines and a cowboy on a ranch in Arizona so, has really seen the country. I can see I've changed a lot in the last year or so. Golly, I used to be so afraid of boys. Well, not <u>really</u> afraid but I'd stutter & stammer around not knowing what to say to them but now I'm different. I sure got rid of my inferiority complex about some

things cuz up here you have to stick up for yourself or you won't get "nut-
tin'." In other words, no one else but yourself looks out for you. But Mom,
don't worry about me getting too forward cuz you know I was brought up
right and will always be a <u>good little girl</u>.

SUNDAY MORN. [MARCH 11]
Yesterday was very uneventful <u>as usual</u>. No one came to visit but I got a
♥ *letter* ♥ *from Ralph last nite so I was satisfied. He went by here in the*
afternoon on his way back from the lab. Gee, I wonder if it's good to have
your heart flutter so. Ha! He really is a swell kid. Friday morning I had Mr.
Reed, our janitor, lug the electric sewing machine down here and after a few
minutes of monkeying around with it, I figured out how to run it. Sure is
slick and I got lots of ripped-out seams in my pj's mended. It's one of those
new portable Singers and so easy to run. Just press down on a little button
to make it run. Think I'll get some goods and a pattern to make me some
p.j.'s or shorts to wear in bed this summer. Joan knows how to read the pat-
terns for directions, etc., so will help me out. Golly, there are so many things
I'd like to do but there just isn't time. Sounds goofy – doesn't it?? I'd love to
do a lot more crocheting, knitting, embroidery work, sewing and drawing
but those darn old lessons take up all my time. It won't be long though til
the State Exam. Joan & I are both feeling super! One of these days we're
going to try to pick up enough courage to ask Dr. Crow if we could go to a
show. Virginia Haley came back day before yesterday. She isn't in the room
next door cuz they put old Grandma Habas in there, and we have to hear
her moan all day long. She's that old Polish lady that can't speak English
who we thought would have passed away long ago.

▧ Margaret Habas was from Czechoslovakia and seventy years old.
  * * *

Boy, we sure have a swell personal nurse now. Mrs. Golberg and she's
"charge" today as this is Rothy's day off. It sure seems like heaven.
P.S. Suppose ya could advance me $1 to hold me over til Easter? All I have
is $.50 left.

MARCH 16, 1945 [FRIDAY]

*Thanks so much for the money. Also thanks for the reprint. We all miss Al
Strom up here so much because he did such wonderful work on developing
films, reprints, etc. Haven't heard lately how he's coming along but he did
have quite a bad hemorrhage.*

Al Strom had been at Riverside Sanatorium near Granite Falls
for five years before coming to Ah-gwah-ching in 1938. He and two
other long-term patients had taken a short course in occupational
therapy and were employed as assistants to Miss Emig. His interest in photography was a boon for patients who had cameras because he operated a film developing lab. Strom had six stages of
thorocoplasty, which was a complete removal of ribs on one side.
A lung hemorrhage was a serious event that could result in death.
Al's prompted John O'Donnell to tell Marilyn about a young girl
who had hemorrhaged so badly that she coughed blood across the
room and died. Marilyn reflected on how odd it seemed to have
the same disease, to potentially be in the same situation, and yet to
talk calmly about such things happening.

* * *

*I'm glad you're selling some of my things, Mom. No, I don't care about that
navy blue sheer dress with the white lace. But please don't sell my aqua
Easter suit. I'd like to have you bring it up when you come so I can see if it
fits after I get up and around. I'll most likely lose some weight as most people do and that old flabby fat will get more solid (I hope!) Joan's folks will
most likely be up again this weekend as her Dad is leaving April 1st to work
at Rosemount in the Cities. He does secretarial work such as bookkeeping.*

Mr. Oseth worked for industries related to the war efforts. He
may have been going to Rosemount to work at the Gopher Ord-
nance Works, a large munitions factory.

* * *

*Carmie never comes around anymore as she's not getting along very good.
She has T.B. throat now so has to be on "silence." Suppose John will be*

coming down the hall any minute now with that precious "local" for me.
Gosh, I'm getting crazier about him (Ralph) every day! Oh-oh! Here comes
John now. (Sigh) – now to continue, if it is at all possible! Well, well, this
really has turned out to be <u>some</u> *nite. Marshall Bex and a Marine friend*
of his just stopped in. For ever cute fellas! The Marine said to me, "Gosh,
are you supposed to be sick?!! You're the healthiest person I've seen since I
got back!" (Hmmmmm) He used a cane so I supposed he was wounded
in action. Didn't want to ask about it because it might have made him
self-conscious.

THURSDAY EVE, MARCH 22, 1945
Oh, what a glorious day this has been!! Our window wide open from top
& bottom and the sun shining. Someone told us it was 69° in the shade
outside. Every day we meet someone new it seems, so I really know most
everyone at "Ching" now. And I just love to meet and talk with . . . well
just <u>people</u> *in general. Mrs. Storlie had her 3rd (and last I hope) stage this*
afternoon. Suppose I'll be hearing from Ralph again tonight. He says he's
just counting the minutes til Easter when I'll be up to see him. Gorsh! Gee,
but I feel super tonight. As happy as a lark! Don't know why. We've seen
so many out walking but it doesn't bother me much cuz I know someday
I'll be doing the same thing and it won't come any faster by feeling sorry
for myself. Even the nurses and doctors have been so perfectly wonderful
lately. Must be the influence of spring. The world seems wonderful when
the nurses just smile a little extra special at you or a doctor gives you an
encouraging word. I think if they knew how this made patients feel they'd
do it more often.

FRIDAY, 13TH [APRIL]
My, we were so shocked at the news of President Roosevelt's death. It was
spread all over the San a few minutes after it came in on the radio. Yester-
day was the darnedest day for things to happen. We heard so much news
– that's why I'm writing you a letter this morn. First of all we were told

by Mary Jo that "Ole" had an examination from Dr. Leggett and she told
her she had to quit working and rest at home in Walker for 2 or 3 weeks
because her resistance is too low and she might come down with the "bug."
She hadn't been feeling or eating good for quite some time so felt quite bad
about it. But it surely is wonderful the way they look after the nurses and
employees to protect them from getting this disease. People really are much
safer working here where they get x-rays every three months than on the
"outside."

■ Nurse Vivian Olson contracted tuberculosis and became a patient. Although several safeguards were in place—including gowns, masks, and handwashing—some employees either developed a new tuberculosis infection or reactivated a previous one.

* * *

Got a letter from Mabel last night and she told me the swell news of her
exam. Her 1st culture came back negative. Isn't that just wonderful? I'm
so happy for her. Her cavity is all closed and she has 1 bathroom privilege
now. Boy, what a thrill!

THURSDAY, APRIL 26, 1945
I'm trying to half listen to Dayton's now while I'm writing this. It's so good
and boy – if I had lots of money the first thing I'd do would be to buy a
record collection. They just played "Stars & Stripes Forever" – my favorite
march. I think I appreciate music even more since I've been here because
I don't have any opportunity to go to concerts, etc. The radio is the only
way we get it. Gosh, I guess I have an awful lot of living to do when I get
home but I'm going to take it plenty easy and get it all done <u>*slow*</u> *but* <u>*sure.*</u>
So many of the patients are getting full privileges and going home. Margie
Popelka, Irene Lahti and several other girls from the B building go over to
the new dining room to eat. Phyllis Tatge is starting to next week.

■ Up until 1945, almost all patients were served meals in their room, putting a burden on dietary staff to deliver meals and nurses to help serve. The new dining room also presented an opportunity

New patient dining room

for a meal privilege, an additional rehabilitation step toward being discharged.

* * *

We sure haven't been having such hot meals of late but that's because of the terrible meat shortage. All we got last week was mutton, liver, and eggs – not one speck of meat. Ugh! And you know how I <u>love</u> all of those three! I'm getting to like eggs pretty well now, though. I guess I told you about Ole having tuberculosis, didn't I? Well, they moved her down to BII with the other patients. She's on the porch just outside Mabel's alcove. It sure is irony – to think that less than 3 weeks ago she was taking care of those same kids that she now is lying next to. They couldn't tell by her x-rays because they were clouded over from the pneumonia so the only way they knew was from her positive sputum. (Just like the way I broke down, isn't it?) When I was coming out of the fluoroscope room yesterday, Dr. Sanderson walked into the room and he said, "Well, well, how's my girl?" and he put his arm *around me. "Sandy" didn't even have a gown or mask on either and you don't know what a wonderful feeling it is when people aren't afraid of you just cuz you have <u>T.B.</u> Oh, how I hate that word – T.B. I think it's even worse than <u>tuberculosis</u>. And when people write on our letters %T.B. San. Grr! We could just wring their pretty necks! Wish they'd just write Ah Gwah Ching, Minn & let it go at that. Ken Farley & Ray Johnson left for home night before last – <u>without consent</u>. Those crazy kids! 'Course Ken was to be discharged in a few weeks so I guess he was okay. He said he was tired of lying around here "eating their macaroni and cheese." John was telling us about that gang of boys upstairs. Harvey Hanson, Glenn Haglund and Polo. Well, as I may have told you, Glenn had a spread & had to take pneumo on both sides. He still is running around with those kids and I hear the doctors are just plenty disgusted with those young guys so they are going to be moved over to DIII. They can't do a thing with them so Dr. Callahan said he was through.*

■ Dissatisfied, recalcitrant, and incorrigible were all labels applied to patients who wouldn't conform to the rules. Usually they were restless young males or older men with alcohol addictions. There was a tuberculosis commitment law, but very few patients were legally committed to a sanatorium; the staff and buildings were not equipped to incarcerate and guard someone. Options for discipline were few and ineffective for patients already confined to their room. Some patients merely arranged for someone to pick them up, and they walked out the door. Others asked for permission to leave, were refused, and left anyway. The doctor would note "left against advice" on the patient's record. Not all runaways healed at home, and some were readmitted. Patients who were a continuing discipline problem were evicted. In all cases, the health department was notified if the patient's sputum was still positive, and he or she was labeled a public health menace.

At Ah-gwah-ching, quarantine quarters were constructed under a 1945 legislative law. This area, located in the E building, at times held federal prisoners who had tuberculosis as well as patients who didn't conform to the rules. In 1955, legislation created a security area at the Anoka State Hospital; the Burns Unit was named after Ah-gwah-ching's former superintendent.

MAY 8, 1945

Last night a little after eight when we were listening to Lux Radio, Miss Weiber, the night snoopervisor, brought up the whole armload of packages from you. Gosh, I was just like a kid opening his Christmas presents – and I sure squealed when I saw those flowers. Boy. I just buried my face way down in them and shut my eyes for a few heavenly seconds. There I was – right back in the woods out by the caves, with the hills and the creek, wiener roasts and the good times we used to have. It will be such a happy day when we can all go out there again. Sometimes I feel that I'm so very lucky to have those wonderful memories – luckier than some people who never realize what a joy the simple things in life are. Like walking through a woods or taking hikes in the hills where you can really get close to nature. Up here, we patients realize it more than ever because we are deprived of so many things. You know – I couldn't have been half as thrilled with those woods flowers if they'd been orchids! Thanks for everything, folks ... I only wish you all could have made yourselves little and hid right inside the boxes, too. Nothing has happened but a little excitement last night. I was just dropping off the deep end when Joan said, "Marilyn, do you hear that noise?" I said no and then she listened again. She screamed, "It's a mouse!" Well then we clicked on the light and there on the window sill was a little mouse peering at us over some books with those little beady eyes! Gosh, the poor thing was more scared than we were and he kept running back & forth on the window sill. Joan was so excited she forgot what she was doing and rang three times (the emergency bell.) I started giggling and Willsie came a running. Honestly, it looked so darn comical – Willsie running around the room trying to hit it with a stick. I almost had hysterics and I laughed so hard the tears just spilled down my cheeks. The little mouse scooted out the door and about ten minutes later we heard Harriet and Vera Hanson making a commotion – it evidently decided to visit them, too. Ha! Oh, I could write a book about this place.

MAY 22, 1945
Right at supper time, Joan got a letter from Virg and he had enclosed some pictures of himself. Joan sat there staring at them and at first wouldn't believe they were him. He looked so terribly changed. You know, that picture of him she has on the wall – well, he was so fat, weighed over 200 lbs. and now he looks so thin and haggard – all tired out. He was in some pretty awful fighting with the 1st army in Germany. Joan just cried and it spoiled her whole supper. Don't mention this to Joan though, cuz she has put them away and doesn't want to look at them. Maybe I'm not even supposed to be telling you all this. I sure wish Ralph could start gaining again. He's been losing weight steadily and when I was up to see him a week ago Sunday night I could notice he was much thinner. His stomach is bothering so he can't eat and he also runs a temp. I can notice his letters aren't as lively as they used to be and, gosh, I wish he would get better soon. His aunt died of T.B. so that was where he got it. Next month his new baby half-brother or sister will be here and is he ever thrilled over it.
[LETTER CONTINUED NEXT MORNING]
Last night I had the worst dream. I dreamed that he died – it was awful. Me and my nightmares. I guess I have death on the brain since Melvin Miner passed away. It really doesn't bother me cuz I'm pretty used to it by now, so don't worry folks.

■ Melvin Miner, who had furnished records for the san's radio program, died on May 19; he was twenty-two years old.

* * *

P.S. Mabel is really going up on the privileges since she got that negative culture. Another priv. every 2 wks. She gets her 3rd one this week.

MAY 26, 1945
Last night Joanie & I put on our nicest blouses and got all dolled up and

after seven the gang arrived. We had potato chips, my ginger ale and root beer. It was fun and we laughed and talked and talked. Then I got out of bed and took some ginger ale over next door to Clara Kowalke and Hildegard Middendorf, her roommate. When I was out in the hall some guys came by and started kidding me about getting "tight." Well, it did look sorta bad – me carrying such a big bottle around. "Ozzie" Osborne took some of the candy, potato chips & ginger ale over to treat Harriet & Vera too. It really was a swell party and I wish we could do it more often.

MONDAY [MAY 28]
Miss Lyford stopped in with my marks on the State Boards – here they are – Eng., perfect score – 195, mine 156. History, perfect score 148, mine 103. It's not so hot, but then considering I really didn't do much studying all year, I guess they could have been worse. Started a little embroidery yesterday – you know I never did really learn how so Joan is showing me the stitches and I'm making that dresser scarf that Betty S and Mary Lou C. gave me for Xmas. Going to be really cute!

TUES. MORN [MAY 29]
Joan's brother, Jim, has been liberated after 3 yrs in a German prisoner camp. She's so happy! They had been waiting to hear for so long.

Jim had been a prisoner of war in Stalag 3B, Fuerstenberg, Brandenburg, Prussia. The camp held 4,222 prisoners, and 4,175 survived their captivity.

* * *

Yesterday I got the class picture & a cute card "To our member" from the Seniors with all their signatures. I just cried I was so happy to see all their faces again & to think they remembered me.

MAY 30, 1945
[MEMORIAL DAY, WHICH WAS ON A WEDNESDAY IN 1945]
Claudis Peterson (he's that blond guy who was Benny's roommate and

now Earl Bemis') well, anyway, last night his mind must have cracked or something because he went out to the wash room and slit his throat with a jack knife. He walked across the hall into Paul Malek's room with the blood squirting all over & fainted. John came down and told us this a few minutes after it happened. Then we were just finishing breakfast this morning when we saw Miss Olson & the charge nurse of BIII run out the side door and across the lawn towards the bushes along our building. It just dawned on Joan & me then that someone had jumped out of the window so I hopped over on her bed and we leaned out the window. Sure enuf, there he was – lying in the peony bushes. It was way down the other end of the hall, though, right above Mrs. Soper's room so she saw him fall. (Guess I forgot to tell you, it was Peterson again, trying to commit suicide). Well, all the charge nurses & orderlies from the D Building rushed out and there must have been at least a dozen nurses out on the lawn. They brought a stretcher and blanket and put him on it. All the while, patients from B, C, & D were hanging out of the windows watching. Whew! My lil ol' heart was going 60 per. We still don't know if he died yet – poor fellow, but I don't see how he could pull through.

▨ Claudis Peterson died two days later, on Friday. He was twenty-seven years old.

* * *

Then (I know this will shock you) Ruby Strand passed away this morning at about 5 o'clock. She had been pretty bad the last few days. Her folks just went by and it was so terribly sad to see them. They didn't get here in time to see her before she went. Mr. Nylander (her father) brought us some lilacs that probably had been for her, and he almost broke down when he said, "Ruby isn't here anymore." Then, on top of all this, Mrs. Ella Gunderson from our floor passed away yesterday morning. She was over on BII after having her 2nd stage in a thoracoplasty. It was her heart, I guess. I didn't know her very well but she was a very nice lady.

13. SUMMERTIME 1945

Oh, how I wish I could be outside!

FRIDAY [JUNE 1]

Yesterday I got a letter from Ray Palmer again. He was 18 in April so now is in the British Army. I'm hoping he'll send me a pic of himself. I really felt a little sick at aspiration & threw up when Dr. Crow had the needle in. I felt so dumb! Haven't thrown up for over a yr.

SATURDAY [JUNE 2]

I'm sending home the package of pajamas today. Hope you can wash them soon, Mom, cuz I sorta need them. Talking about things I need – suppose you could "reimburse me financially?" My, what big words! I sent to Sears with Joan's order to get a cute sewing box so I'm a little low on cash right now. And say, what do you think about me buying a slack suit? I'm sure Aunt Ruth would get me one in the Cities – one that I could use both in summer & winter.

MONDAY [JUNE 4]

We got a new "crew" on the floor today, beginning the new month. We have Lois Mason, a young nurse. We'll get weighed this aft., but I hope I stay the same – 126. Joan's folks get enuf gas from the ration board to drive up once a month by just seeing the family doctor about it. Wish you could find out about that in St. Peter, Daddy. Of course, they get it because the bus & train connections aren't as good between Alex and here. But then it takes so long for you to come by bus and that way you'd have to take off an extra day so that should be a good reason. Hope you can send me about $5 soon *cuz I owe Joanie $2.45 for that stuff we sent away for, and she also paid for me for the memorial funds for Ruby and Mrs. Gunderson.*

SUNDAY NITE [UNDATED LETTER, PROBABLY JUNE 10]
Oh. I have been so happy these last few days. There have been so many things going on we haven't had a dull moment. Joan's mother, dad, sister Jackie, brother Bill, & Joey were all here from about noon til a little after supper. They are such swell people and so nice to me. They gave Joan & I each a big box of Johnston's chocolates. Her brother Bill – aged 20 – is so cute! He brought Joanie a beautiful pair of sparkly earrings from Fountain-bleu (or however you spell it) and her sister got a cute charm bracelet from France with the coat of arms of several cities. He's home for a 30-day furlough and they are hoping Jim, the one who was a P.O.W. will be home soon so they can all come up again. Joan went outside to see Joey for a while and when they came back Bill was pushing her in the wheelchair so he told me to hop on too for a ride. I didn't quite know if I dared but everyone was out of bed this afternoon watching the ball game and I already had my house coat on so I sat on Joan's lap, He wheeled us way to the end of the BII hall and we stopped and talked with different ones before

Roommate Joan with brothers and sister

coming back. It was fun and no one said anything to me. The sun finally
came out yesterday so they had the ball game, and prisoners won over the
employees 12 to 0. Isn't that a terrific score? We were very ashamed of them
but they are all 4F'ers and the cons are such young healthy guys. Vivian Ol-
son's folks were out here Saturday afternoon and they brought her a log of
beautiful lilies so she sent a beautiful bouquet over to Joan & me. Mmmm
– they smell so wonderful. We have a lot of flowers in our room, quite a few
bright little plants lining our window sills and it makes the room so much
more homey. Honestly we've been having more "men" visitors the last few
nites. Art Sabotke [Sabatke] said to us last night, "Whenever you hear any
guys on CII, you can be sure they're down in Shippey and Barnes' room"

■ Art had been at Ah-gwah-ching for several years and was part of
that group of older men who played cribbage and cards and went
visiting.

* * *

Saturday nite Don & Glenn were talking to us through the window about
eight-thirty and handing us a line – as usual! They always yell "Hey honey,
stick your pretty little head out" or "Okay, sweetheart" and you know all
that rot! They asked us if we wanted some beer and they'd send it down on
a string. We told them "No, no!" but pretty soon here comes a beer bottle
dangling down and we were just petrified cuz probably the whole B & D
building were watching. So I reached out and grabbed it before too many
saw it and then a second bottle came down. We kept telling them "no" but
they did it all the more because they knew how embarrassed we were. Well,
we didn't know what to do with it so we asked Mabel Jones next door to
come over and she drank some. (I cannot tell a lie, Father, as little George
Washington said) Yes, I poured out a little for myself just to try it but ugh!
It was so ishy I threw it out the window in the grass. We hope none of the
big shots saw us but then beer is allowed here, and it's really supposed to be
good for you. It was just the idea of it though, that we didn't like.

■ Beer was allowed at Ah-gwah-ching, especially for people who
didn't like to drink milk. Made from grain, it contains many of the

same nutrients, such as B vitamins, riboflavin, niacin, zinc, potassium, and calcium.

* * *

We heard there were to be some new rules put into effect soon by Dr. Callahan and they're going to start being real strict. (My gosh, I wouldn't doubt it after that popcorn party & beer bottle deal of ours!) I doubt very much if they could change things because they have no one to enforce the rules if they made them. Certainly grown men & women aren't going to take orders from these inexperienced nurses' aides who are mere <u>kids</u> and don't know <u>half</u> as much about T.B. as the patients themselves. I don't think they'll really get strict til after the war when the R.N.s & trained nurses come back to work here. However, they might do some changing around in the different buildings. We heard they are going to make CII a "sick floor" and move all the patients who are getting along okay and feel good (like us!) over to the B building. In a way, I sorta hope it doesn't happen cuz I'm afraid I'd miss my "private" room. I was just wishing I'd get my slack suit and what d'ya know? Here comes a big box for me in the mail from Mpls. Oh, honestly, I just about died with joy at the beautiful things Aunt Ruth picked out for me! The slack suit is a beautiful lime green called "lettuce green" – a new shade this spring and it fits me beautifully. I asked her to send me a blouse with a tie in front and she did. It matches nicely – it's a rayon candy stripe. Real darling! Also she sent me some flowers for my hair of the same color as the slacks. Now comes the sad part of it – the price— (please be sure and count ten, Daddy) $8.95 for the slack suit - $3.00 for the blouse and $1.00 for the 2 clusters of artificial flowers. I think that is very reasonable in this day & age and they are lovely things. Gosh, I haven't had any new "clothes" (really clothes) for so long it's really a treat. And, as you all know – I'm so crazy about "nice" things – more than ever now.

WEDNESDAY MORNING [JUNE 13]
Thought today I'd send you our new rules and regulations. Yeah, man, now we live in a regular "prison."

■ The "Information and Rules for Patients" expanded on Dr. Callahan's previous list. Some detailed instructions were added, including:

> Do not lick stamps or wet your finger in your mouth to turn the pages of a book.
>
> Do not offer food to visitors or employees.
>
> Care of artificial teeth. In removing teeth handle them with paper napkins, not with bare fingers.
>
> Hold a paper tissue over your nose and mouth when laughing or talking.

On the copy Marilyn sent home she wrote, *I might as well just wear a mask and be done with it, for all the gabbing I do. Ha!*

* * *

We heard from one of the nurses that they really are going to make CII the infirmary <u>and soon</u>. So maybe even this week we'll be moved to either BII or CIII. Gosh, the more I think of it the less I like it. We don't even know if Joanie & I will get together. Yesterday I was wanting to be home but today I'm happy again. Just goes by streaks.

WEDNESDAY [JUNE 14]

I was aspirated this afternoon instead of morning and we had Callahan instead of Crow because he's down to the U with a patient. Sure went slick. He never hurts you a bit. My fluid was so clear that he said I won't have another series of penicillin because I don't need it.

■ The April issue of *The Moccasin* quoted Marilyn as saying that having those rounds of penicillin treatments was just like having a privilege because she was able to go gadding every morning.

SATURDAY [JUNE 16]

I just heard from Roberta and she's wanting to come up with you folks so much next week. She may not get up if she doesn't come then so please, can she come along? I'm counting on seeing her because it's been so long since

I've seen any of the "kids." It would be nice if one of the other girls could come too to keep her company (like Nadine or Agatha) but then there probably wouldn't be room. I can hardly wait to see you all.

MONDAY MORN [JUNE 18]

Last night Mabel Bakalar came over to see me and we had a nice visit. She doesn't giggle half as much but still talks awfully loud. She must be growing up now that she's past 18. After we had been closed up for the nite we were so hungry. Just like an answer to our prayer, Don Moen hollered down and asked us if we wanted some hot egg sandwiches – that they were making them up in their rooms and would send them down with Sue Mosher, the nurse. Boy, they were luscious! Those fellas sure know how to cook. Mabel Jones came over Friday night and we cut out my pajamas. I've started basting on them and probably will get them finished the week after you get here. We have a new patient on our floor and she's just about driving everybody nuts. She's in Ruby Strand's old room so it's nice & close. She yells at the nurses all day & all night for attention. The patients are all going to complain to Doc Cal & Crow so we can have something done about it – get her put in some other kind of institution or sumpin'!

P.S. Wish you could take me for a car ride when you're here but I'm afraid that's pretty impossible.

TUESDAY MORNING [JUNE 19]

Uncle Gerold, Aunt Ruth, Mrs. Anderson, and Helen arrived at 2 o'clock yesterday afternoon and we had a lovely visit. I went over to the reception room and stayed until they went at around 4. Showed them the library & new patients' dining room – saw Nancy & Bev outside the window. They have grown so. They brought me a big box of oranges, bananas, plums, tomatoes, & cherries.

■ Marilyn's parents came to visit and stayed at a resort for a long weekend.

THURSDAY [JUNE 28]

It's been quiet around Ching since you left but I've been reading and sleeping a lot. The sticky, rainy weather makes us all so lazy. Yesterday I was aspirated and it was pretty slick. Only about an ounce of fluid. Have to get at some letters today. I owe so many and no wonder I don't get any mail lately.

JULY 1ST, SUNDAY

Dear Mom & Grandma,

The letter was addressed to Grandma Barnes, who was making her annual visit in St. Peter. Grandma Laumann and Nita went to Minneapolis for a visit, and Marilyn's dad and brother were at Scout camp.

* * *

By the time you get this I suppose you'll be all alone. Boy, I bet it will seem funny with Grams & Nita and Daddy and Keith all away. Those pictures sure turned out nice! I especially like the one of Keith & me standing on that sidewalk by the pines and so did a lot of others. Joan is having her extra-pleural this coming Thursday or Friday so I'm gonna be all alone. Boo Hoo! Talk about changes being made! Here are a few on the nursing staff: Miss Hoff left, so now Mrs. Bowen who was her assistant will take over as Supt. of Nurses. Then Miss Olson (charge on BII) will be Bowen's assistant and Reece will be charge on BII. Miss Rosenquist on CIII is going to change places as charge with Mrs. Reed (our janitor's wife) on EIV (where the little Indian kids are). We have only 20 patients and not real sick since Mrs. Hagen died last night. She's that woman who had T.B. spine and hollered all the time. About 8:30 p.m. last night Weiber (the nite snoop) came by and shut all our doors so they could wheel Mrs. Hagen down to the morgue. Seems to me they could have at least waited til after we were closed up for the night! But gosh, so much stuff like that goes on here, it just doesn't affect me any more – I'm so used to it. Oh have we been having terrible meals the last three days!! The worst concoctions. Why, I couldn't even dream 'em up in a nightmare! Honest, the food isn't so bad but the way it's prepared. Black

Keith with Marilyn, who is wearing her lettuce green slack suit

lumpy potatoes, cold "shadow" soup, eggs, eggs, and more eggs – and you know how fond I am of them especially when they are scrambled in lard, etc.

■ Shadow soup is chicken soup so tasteless that patients claimed the chicken was just waved over the soup pot.

* * *

After dinner –

Well, well, here I just get through griping about food and we have ham, scalloped corn, cracked wheat bread & butter, mashed potatoes, candied prunes, pineapple sherbet & angel food cake for dinner (the cake was a treat from Solveig). I really enjoyed myself – had seconds on everything – even sherbet, so made up for the "starvation diet" the first of this week.

■ Solveig Ohman was a thirty-two-year-old married woman whose daughter, Joyce, age twelve, died at Ah-gwah-ching in August of 1944.

SUNDAY NITE—

I'll have to write and tell you of the visitors I had this afternoon. First of all, Agnes Olson and Olive Peterson from St. Peter came in. They were awfully nice to stop in.

■ Agnes Olson was the piano teacher in St. Peter. A benefit of being in resort country was the number of visitors stopping by in the summer.

* * *

Then later on a distinguished looking man walked by. He looked in and then I heard him ask where Marilyn Barnes was. It just dawned on me that it was Ralph's dad cuz I had seen pictures of him. He brought me some cherries. Gosh, I was so flustered – I didn't know what to say. He was very handsome – he and Ralph look almost like brothers. He didn't stay long as he'd just come and wanted to get back to CIII, but when he went out he said he'd see me again. John stopped in before dinner to tell me that Ralph was feeling "in the pink." Temp normal 'n everything so I could expect a 5-page letter tonight. My, my! I've turned over a new leaf! The only time I get out of bed is when it's being made in the morning. Boy, am I getting good!

JULY 3, 1945 [TUESDAY]

Keith and Daddy, [at camp]

Everything goes on the same as ever at "Ching." Only we have a new bunch of "green" nurses on the floor and are they dillies! One big lady who we call "Minnie" is a card! She gets all our names mixed up but she's such a jolly thing. She doesn't even know how to make hospital corners on our beds. Say – I bet you have to make them on your cots out there too, huh?

■ A hospital corner is the fold on a flat bedsheet made by tucking the sheet straight under the mattress and then making a diagonal fold at the side corner of the sheet and tucking it under to produce a triangular corner. In the days before fitted sheets, this process made a smooth, secure corner that held the sheet in place. The practice probably came to nursing through the profession's initial relationship with the military, the legend being that new recruits had to make their bedding so flat and tight that a dropped quarter would bounce off it.

JULY 3, 1945 [TUESDAY]

I got the box of P.J.'s yesterday. Thanks a lot for washing them. I hope I can finish my new ones soon cuz I need them. Wish you could send me a couple more pairs because I could really use them. Rayon ones are the only kind you can get nowadays.

JULY 5, 1945 [THURSDAY]

Well, it's the big day today! At about 12 noon Joan will be going down for surgery. She had an enema yesterday aft. and a sleeping pill last night but she's feeling just as chipper as anything this morning. She couldn't have any breakfast & no dinner and they'll shave her back and give her a morphine hypo later on this morning. Boy, this prep stuff is really an ordeal! I'll have to tell you about our "4th" celebration. Well, we really had fun and it seemed different from just any other day at Ching. The prisoners & San employees had a baseball game from 2 to 4 in the afternoon. I got a ringside seat in Hildegard's room – sat on her chair by the window and John brought us Cokes after a while.

▪ This summer would be the last for the prisoner/employee games. The program with St. Cloud Prison was discontinued, mostly because when the farm bought tractors there was less need for labor—no horses to care for and feed. Also, three prisoners trusted not to escape stole a visitor's car and drove to Little Falls, where they were captured.

* * *

It was "open house" all day and lots of patients went visiting. Well, Ralph wrote me a note and asked me to come up so – I tho't heck! I'd just get up enuf nerve to do it. So I put on my "lettuce green" slack suit and asked "Smitty" our new nurse to take me at seven. No one asked where I was going cuz everyone was visiting, too, and I just sat on a chair and talked – the same as I would have down here on CII anyway. Gosh, it was fun. Ralph is feeling much better and he & Palmer, his roommate, are two crazy nuts. We really had a swell visit and it was really a scream when I was trying to teach them how to crochet.

FRIDAY MORN. [JULY 6]
Joan's dad visited with me all the time she was down at surgery yesterday and he is so nice. She was down there exactly 3 hours. When they wheeled her past she looked in and smiled and said, "hi." They all say she's getting along fine and I'm so glad. Her dad is staying several days and maybe tomorrow or the next day her brothers will be up as Bill has to report back to camp soon.

JULY 12, 1945 [THURSDAY]
I talked to Al Strom about making reprints and gave him the negatives. He sent for some developing paper of that size picture so they'll be just the same as those you sent me. I'm having $2.00 worth made so I sure could use a little "moola." When they are .04 apiece, it really mounts up. Ralph has a new baby brother. "Butch" as he calls him, was born Sunday July 8th and weighed 8 lbs, 12 oz. Pretty nice and is he thrilled.

SATURDAY [JULY 14]
It's a beautiful sunny morning today and oh, how I wish I could be outside! Gosh, that wonderful fresh pine air does wonders for a person. If only they had porches that we could sit out on. I heard from Joan and she's feeling swell except she's still quite sore which is to be expected. She'll probably come "home" day after tomorrow or the next day. I can hardly wait. Heard from Irene Lahti last night and she's expecting to get a government position

possibly out of state. She's having a wonderful time getting acquainted with her family again.

■ Marilyn received a postcard from Irene Lahti with a view of the North Shore Drive and Lake Superior north of Two Harbors. Irene mentioned taking a civil service exam in Duluth and asked Marilyn to say "Hi" to some other patients.

SUNDAY AFTERNOON, JULY 15, 1945

Lou Ann Ost popped in on me for a visit. She got here last night and will go back tomorrow night. I could tell she feels quite bad that her mother is so thin now and failing steadily. Last night I had the best time when I visited on BII. The nurses and kids are so swell on that floor – I sure wouldn't mind being over there. I visited with Viv Olson and Rita Steinhagen Saturday nite too and those kids are more fun.

■ Rita Steinhagen entered a convent in 1951 and took vows as a Sister of St. Joseph of Carondelet. Sister Rita considered herself a peaceful activist and spent time in a federal penitentiary at age seventy for protesting at Fort Benning, Georgia.

* * *

Aunty Ruth sent me some pretty rayon satin pajamas but they were way too big. I'm going to ask around here if anyone would like to buy them first before I send them back and have her get the next smaller size.

[CONTINUED ON MONDAY]

It was hard to go to sleep last night when it was light outside so Hildegard next door and the two boys up above me and I talked until a quarter to ten. A nice breeze came up and it was so heavenly – the moon was shining, too. A pity it had to be wasted. I just love the nights up north – they always cool off – near a lake anyway – and all the different sounds – like the loons and crickets & frogs & the pines stirring in the breeze.

TUESDAY [JULY 17]

Well, I sold the pajamas to Miss Jones, our nurse, so I won't have to send them back. She was glad to buy them because they are impossible to find around Walker. Y'know, we're just "up in the sticks." One of these days when I get a few more pieces of fancywork done I'll have Miss Emig launder them & then will send them home, for you to keep for me. Some of these things I want you to put away in the closet where I have all of my other "hope chest" things.

THURSDAY [JULY 19]
Joan came back yesterday morning & is just the same as ever although she lost a few pounds. We really had a gab fest and how! Right now she's down stairs for aspiration and pneumo. I hope she doesn't have much or <u>any</u> fluid. I heard from Mable B. who is home now. She says it's just like a dream!

THURSDAY MORN. [AUGUST 2]
Boy, are we all sleepy today. They moved that crazy woman in next door where Clara & Hildegarde used to be and she hollered and screamed steadily all night until at 4 o'clock some bright nurse decided it was about time to give her a shot of morphine. I fell asleep about 4:30 and then wash water came at 6, so - - - Our janitor just came in and is washing the walls of our room today so he moved me out in the hall. I'm between Fanchon F's room & Hildegarde's down near the runway to BII. Is it ever fun out here in the hall – you can see so much going on and I can talk to both of the kids.

[LETTER MISSING FROM AUGUST 6; HAVE ENVELOPE]

TUESDAY [AUGUST 7]
We don't get hardly any flowers at all. Mr. Waddell is too busy and no one else brings us any. Sure would love some, esp. gladiolas.

THURSDAY [AUGUST 9]
Do you know, I sent for some crochet cotton to Wards and yesterday got a check back. <u>Permanently out of stock</u>. So wish you'd look all through

the St. Peter stores for some size 30 or 40 in any pretty shaded colors – 3 balls. 3 balls of yellow I need to make that "thing" for your dining room, Mom. I like shaded colors for crocheting around embroidered pieces. They finally got rid of Mrs. Swenson that crazy woman next door. Her husband came and got her yesterday afternoon and what a relief. Got a wonderful night's rest last night. She screamed so loud that everyone in the whole San. heard her.

14: PRIVILEGES AND LESSONS

It seems just natural to be walking

AUGUST 11, 1945

Well, we are all waiting anxiously for the news of surrender. Some excitement, eh what? We just stay glued to our earphones. But it just doesn't seem to mean as much to us stuck up in this place because we seem so far away from war and the same old routine goes on whether or not. Now if I were home it would be different cuz there people can shout and show their excitement while here we just take it all calmly and quietly talk about it. No celebration. Yesterday during afternoon rest hour I couldn't sleep and I was day dreaming of the first time I come home again. Oh golly, I pictured just how everything would be & look and how it would feel walking up that little curved sidewalk to the door and Daddy would be sitting in the big chair and the rest of you sitting around listening to the radio or talking. It sure was a letdown when I opened my eyes & found I was still in the room.

SUNDAY NIGHT [AUGUST 12]

Got those beautiful glads yesterday (Sat.) at 4 p.m. and oh, thanks loads! Everyone just raved about them and I haven't seen anything like them for ages it seems. Am cutting off the stems and changing their water every day so hope they last a while. Well, we are still waiting for the surrender news broadcast. Say, how about advancing me a little "moola"? I need a little extra so I can pay Florence. Thanks. It seems that I always put my "requests" at the last. Ha!

TUESDAY MORN, 10 A.M. [AUGUST 14]

I've been listening to the radio all morning so just now started my writing. Gosh, isn't it exciting? We were pretty disappointed Sunday nite when we heard that news flash was a false alarm. I sure hope it really will be over today. Yesterday I went to chapel with Tess Paulson and Mrs. Storlie. A very nice service and afterwards I stood out in the hall talking with Mr. Snyder. He said he'll be coming down to visit me one of these Saturdays. Sig Haugen took me home – the <u>long</u> way – via CIII so we stopped and talked – of course – with Bemis & Ralph. Awfully nice of Sig. He's a patient on CIV, up on full privilege. Lately he's been taking over John O'D's "mail route" cuz John hasn't been feeling up to it. Heart trouble, I guess.

MY LUCKY DAY!! AUGUST 15, 1945 [WEDNESDAY]

Well, I guess no one could be any happier than "Miss Lindy Barnes" today! Guess what?? I had my 3 months checkup from Doc Crow this afternoon <u>and</u> . . . he gave me One Bathroom Privilege – how I love that man!! Oh gosh, it's such a thrill . . . no one realizes until they've been kept strict in bed for almost 2 years. I'm so happy I feel like just getting up and shouting "I have a privilege!" to everyone that goes by. Wouldn't it sound dumb to outsiders, tho'? They'd sure think I was a crackpot to be so excited over just being able to walk to the bathroom once a day. "Doc" said I sure am doing okay for myself and didn't mention a thing more about surgery – even when I asked him. I've been negative for a long time and he's going to give me another series of 3 bottles for a test. If they are all negative I might (notice I say <u>might</u>) get a culture. My temp is just swell and he said if this privilege doesn't raise my temp or give me any ill effects he'll give me the 2nd privilege before long, too. Wowie!! I could just sing!! My air space is closed as far as he can see and he thinks he will only have to aspirate me a couple more times – then might not get anything. Next Wednesday is my aspiration day so I hope-a-hope!! I'm gonna take it plenty easy now that he's put me up on a little exercise and I'm not going to overdo just cuz I'm getting along so well. Because I've seen how so many others have broken down *again and I wouldn't want that to happen to me. Although being promoted from strict bed to one privilege means an awful lot. Now I'll be able to go to a show occasionally and visiting and maybe to church services. If I get two privileges, I may even be able to go home for a visit like Mabel did. Oh boy . . . wouldn't that be wonderful! It seems just like a dream!!!! Oh, wasn't the news wonderful last night? When they announced that the war was over on the radio, everyone on CII yelled "Whoopee" and we could hear all the patients in B & D hollering across the lawn. "The War is over!!" Everyone was just overjoyed and after 7 we had an "illegal" open house so everyone went around visiting. I wish they'd have a V.J. Day church service in the chapel because I'd love to go. But no one will have time to come out here I suppose – we're sorta the "forgotten people" when this excitement is on in other places.*

■ The nurses and orderlies ran out of the building and celebrated, yelling and jumping and letting off steam, remembered Marilyn. "And there we were, stuck in our beds and couldn't do anything to express the same emotion."

* * *

Gee, the world seems pretty darn wonderful to me today. It seems like I'm really started on the road home now. Joan & I have been listening to the band music and patriotic programs on the radio all day. I think I love band music better than anything else. It makes me feel just like marching and I can imagine myself going through the motions and fingerings of playing my flute. But one good thing – even if I can never play it again I can always enjoy listening to music. I'm going to write a note to Ralph telling him about my privilege now so better sign off. By the way, we don't write to each other regularly any more.

THURSDAY [AUGUST 16]
Yesterday Joan & I went down for aspiration at the same time. We both got aspirated and neither of us had much fluid. The elevator in our building was out of order so we had to go the "long way home" via BII.

■ Marilyn remembered being thrilled with these detours. The constant confinement transformed ordinary things into major events.

* * *

After I had just gotten back up stairs Kittleson came up and handed me a sputum bottle and said, "Well, you got a privilege and now you've got a <u>culture</u>!" Was I surprised. Doc Crow didn't even order the 3 concentrates (regular sputum tests) before this so he must have been kinda sure. Oh, Mom and Dad – if I can only pass the culture test!! I'm not going to build my hopes up too high and I don't want you to either because it's a terrible disappointment when they come back positive. But if it comes back negative – <u>if</u> – then you can expect me home in the spring. Doctor Crow will no doubt put me up on more privileges as the time goes along anyway but if I get a negative culture then I'd get full privileges (taking my own tub bath, etc.) and outdoor exercise. Doesn't it sound just heavenly? Boy, I can hardly wait to see you and get some fresh fruit and vegetables. Honestly we're just starved for them. We don't get half enuf fruit up here so could you please bring some? And we haven't gotten <u>any</u> fresh vegetables all summer. I don't understand it and I think it's a <u>crime</u>! Things must not grow at all in their gardens up here. Our mouths just water for sweet corn and peas.

AUGUST 18, 1945, SATURDAY
Well, I just got back from the bathroom so now will attempt a little letter-writing. Yesterday was my first day but I had to go in the wheelchair both ways. Today they took me down there and I walked back with Hildegarde. It's nice I have someone young to pal with. We are the only two kids who have privileges. – all the rest are older married women. I talk to Valborg, Molly Frame, Solveig Ohman, and Tess Paulson every day – it's a lot of fun and sure seems wonderful to be able to stand up and really wash good and brush my teeth and go to the "biffy." The bathroom window looks out towards the woods so we sit there and talk and that fresh morning air is <u>wonderful</u>! It seems just natural to be walking and I don't feel weak or

short of breath at all. My pulse goes up a bit though, which is to be expected when I've been in bed so long.

TUESDAY MORN. [AUGUST 21]
I think it's swell that you're bringing Roberta along on Labor Day. Also hope Mory and Sharon can come too. Joan is feeling much better so I think the fluid is going away. I talked with "Ole" the other day and she got her first privilege the day before I got mine. She'll be going to the show with me Aug. 30th, too. Goody!

AUGUST 24TH [FRIDAY]
Thursday nite I was over at Fanchon's and we sat in the window and had quite a gab session with the boys upstairs. "Duke," Ralph, Palmer, and that handsome Nistler guy were all in Ralph's room. We were begging for something to eat cuz we were so hungry so finally they sent down some popcorn on a string. We had quite a time but finally got it. Some nite Earl Bemis is going to lend us his hot plate and we're gonna fry some eggs and maybe hamburgers if Tess Paulson can get some in town. Say, I wonder if

you could bring me some Spam or somepin' like that. Or does it cost too many red points? If it does, just skip it.

■ In 1943, the US Office of Price Administration decided to ration canned goods. The food was needed for troops

Fanchon Fischer demonstrated how patients used their windows to communicate

overseas, and the cans used scarce metals. Each person was allocated ration stamps worth so many points. Red stamp points were for meats, butter, fat, and oils.

* * *

I wish you could find me some cute novel stationery in the Cities or Kato. I am so tired of writing on this plain stuff and now all I have left is this tablet paper. I certainly wish people would send me stuff like they did the first year. Golly – listen to me!! But I can always use 3 things no matter how much I get and they are – pajamas, stationery, & stamps!

AUGUST 27TH [MONDAY]

Joan & I just decided that we're not going to give or rather make presents for all the relatives & friends this year. Just for our immediate family. I hope you'll tell the folks. I just can't do it again this year. After all, I'm here to get well and there is enough excitement at Christmastime. Saw Mrs. Storlie in the bathroom this morning and she said she'll probably be going home next month. Harvey Hanson followed Glenn Haglund by being "kicked out" last week.

TUESDAY MORN. [AUGUST 28]

Gee, thanks so much for the corn & tomatoes. I got the box yesterday morn (Mon.) at 10 o'clock so we had some for both dinner & supper. Sure delish! And those tomatoes are real stuff – not like these green shipped in kind we get up here. Oh yes—about my temp and pulse since I've had this privilege – well, they go up a little more, naturally, after not walking for so long. But it's nothing to be scared of, because everyone's does and it's not even high enough to be called a real thing.

WEDNESDAY NITE [AUGUST 29]

Miss Lyford came around this afternoon and told me I'd be starting lessons next week – ugh. So I really have done half the things I wanted to this summer. Didn't finish my p.j.'s but now that Mabel Jones is back again she'll help me. You are coming Sat. night, aren't you? Got a card from Aunt Peg this morning saying they'd come Saturday. Goody! Mrs. Storlie is moving over to DII in the wards one of these days now cuz she's on full privilege and will be going to the dining room. They are going to make CII the surgery floor this fall (next month) so are going to have to move some patients to BII. Most likely will be those who have privileges – wonder who? We'll find out in the next few days.

■ Marilyn's family visited over Labor Day weekend.

TUESDAY [SEPTEMBER 4]

There won't be much to write today after our long visit but suppose I should drop you a card anyway. We sure had a good time, didn't we? And I en-

Marilyn's family stayed at a resort:
Aunt Nita, Virginia, Bill, Keith, and Tippy

joyed that wheelchair ride so much. When you left yesterday I guess I forgot to thank you for all the things but you knew I meant well anyway. Thanks, Grandma (B) for the stamps – I sure can always use them, and Keith, I sure liked the hair band. More rumors going around now about the moving, cuz docs Cal, Crow & Leggett were here yesterday counting off rooms. Golly, I bet something will really happen today. Surgery starts in a few weeks or sooner so they'll have to do something soon. We are still enjoying the fruit & tomatoes – boy, I'm eating like a horse – weighed 129 yesterday afternoon.

SATURDAY [SEPTEMBER 8]

Boy, this sure is a dreary day. Windy, dark, and rainy and last night we had quite a bad storm. Day before yesterday I gave Al Strom the film so he could develop it so I imagine I'll get it back today.

MONDAY EVE. [SEPTEMBER 10]

From now on I guess I'll be writing to you in the evening cuz that is my only "free" time. You see, I study an hour in the morning and an hour in the aft. and rest hours and interruptions take up the rest. Won't get much fancywork done at this rate but then I'm not going to try.

SEPT. 13, 1945 [THURSDAY]

Yesterday was Ruthie Jones' birthday (also John O'D's) so nite before last Joan & I had a party for her in our room. Well, that night she and her roommate Tess Paulson came over and we had root beer and Spam-wiches, and we played Chinese checkers with me as the winnah! Solveig & Hilde stopped in for a while, too. Then last night Jonesy invited us all over to her big room and we had coffee & doughnuts. Very delicious! The whole crowd was there – Shall I tell you who all? Molly Frame, Solveig, Jonesy of course, Tess, Mrs. Lockrem, Joan, Mabel Jones, and myself. What a time! Molly Frame is such a cut-up and so we were kept laughing most of the time. The party broke up at quarter to nine and we scooted back "home" to bed – but

Joan and I couldn't sleep so we talked til eleven. Come to think of it – I was the only single girl there – all the rest married. But I don't feel out of place with them cuz they're all so friendly & full of fun. Naturally our main topic was this moving business. They are going to empty quite a few rooms on this floor for surgery which is starting the middle of next week. We expect to be thrown out of our rooms any minute cuz the moving will start today or tomorrow and no one knows just who is to be moved. I kind of hate thinking of it because now our bunch will be separated. Valborg Storlie is going home the last of the week because her culture came back negative and she's been up on exercise as you know. Also Hildegarde Middendorf is being moved to DII wards soon. She'll move as soon as she gets a brace on her back – I guess she has a vertebrae out of place or something. Yesterday I was aspirated and I still have fluid but it's getting harder and harder for Doc Crow to get in with the needle – my air space is so small. Not much fluid either.

Some CII gals: Jonesy, Joan, Tess, Rose

SEPT. 15TH [SATURDAY]

It's almost dinner time and we are anxiously awaiting a "good" dinner of corn and tomatoes. Oh boy!! Thanks so much for sending it, folks, we sure love corn and tomatoes – never seem to get our fill. By the way – they all came okay through the mail – we kept the two pears in our room while the rest was put in the kitchen. Last night we were surprised when Valborg came down to say "good bye." Mr. Storlie came for her unexpectedly so last night they left together on the midnight train. I'm so happy for her. Joan's husband is supposed to be on a ship coming home now. In the papers it said his outfit was to sail from LeHavre, France, yesterday (the 14th).

MONDAY [SEPTEMBER 17]

There isn't much news except that some of the moving is starting today – just on the floor. The rest will be on Wed. So far they haven't said anything to us so we're not worrying about it. Have my 1st lesson this afternoon and I have all my studies done – for once!! Senior English is easy for me and I enjoy this English literature much more than I did Am. Hist. last year. Social is kinda hard tho' – such hard reading, big words, etc. But I'm struggling along as best I can.

SUNDAY AFT. [SEPTEMBER 23]

This morning we had more activity cuz since next Thursday the first surgery starts, everything was moved up a day so we get baths today instead of tomorrow and Sunday will be our bath day from now on. Speaking of this surgery – we're going to have 3 men on our floor. Hmmm! This noon we had such a good dinner. Steak, potatoes and gravy, fried onions, sliced tomatoes, bread, butter, and milk. Then for dessert I had two *big dishes of vanilla ice cream cuz some one didn't want theirs. Only thing tho – I sure could have gone for a piece of your luscious chocolate cake, Mom. I do wish I could come home for a vacation this fall before the weather gets too cold. The more I think of it the more I want to – I could have all my favorite dishes etc. – and I know I'd be much more satisfied to come back. It will* be two years next month since I've been home – sure wish you'd write the doctors about it. I'd love to be home for my birthday but maybe that's too soon. We've been getting quite a few tomatoes from the gardens lately so you won't have to send us any more. I sure could go for some cookies, though. We're all out of sweets to nibble on between meals when we get hungry. Did I tell you how much I enjoyed the show last week? It was "An American Romance" with Brian Donlevy taking the lead and it was all about how he, a foreigner, came to the U.S. at the first of the century and how he came to Minnesota and worked in the iron mines up on the Mesabi. It was all in Technicolor. This week, "Thirty Seconds Over Tokyo" starring Van Johnson is on and both Joan & I are going to ask to go.

[LATER:]

Were we ever surprised! Mr. and Mrs. Oseth, Jim, and Jacqueline came at about 4 o'clock so we had company after all. Jim was in civilian clothes – the first time Joan had seen him out of uniform for 6 years. Did he look cute! He's going to Dunwoody in Mpls. starting next week. His fiancé is entering the U this fall so they'll be down there together.

P.S. I do want to come home!!

15. CHANGES

Everything was in such a dither

MONDAY [OCTOBER 1]

Joan's husband is terribly sick at home, has pneumonia and they think maybe it's T.B. They'll get the report back on the sputum tests Tues. or Wednesday – isn't that terrible? Her husband doesn't have anything to go on because he's been steadily going down for so long and Joan is worried sick. None of his folks even knew him when he got off the train in Alex. Joan doesn't sleep hardly at all at nite and is so blue thinking of it all day long. I just don't know what to do or say to cheer her up. Kinda hard. Wish she could go home if it would make her feel any better.

■ Virg Shippey had been in the Battle of the Bulge and then was in a German prisoner of war camp. He knew he was sick, but he believed that if he complained about being ill he would be admitted to a hospital in Europe and not be shipped home to the United States. By the time he reached Minnesota, he was near death.

* * *

Last night I went down to see Harriet – had to get away from this room. Has Dad written to the doctors about me going home to have my teeth fixed? One of my fillings that he put in 2 weeks ago is out already. So many that are negative are going home to have dental work done.

OCTOBER 4, 1945 [THURSDAY]

I know you have been anxious to hear from me; all about my birthday and everything but everything has been so upset I haven't had time until now. You see, Virg, Joan's husband, died yesterday morning at 6 o'clock. Her mother and father came right away and she was called down to the doctor's office at 3 in the afternoon and they broke the sad news to her. It was just terrible!! Dr. Crow and Miss St. John came up and told me that I'd know what had happened when Joan came back to the room. I just bawled in front of them because I knew how terrible Joan felt, and I'm so close to her. We had been so happy in the morning and everyone was saying "Happy Birthday" to me and Dr. Crow was clowning down at aspiration – saying he was going to give me "the works." Then I came back to the room and opened up all my presents from you. Gee, thank you all so much – I had such a wonderfully happy birthday – in the morning anyway. We had planned on a little party with ice cream and cake for yesterday afternoon so when Solveig and Lucy Niesen came in the wheelchair from BIII, I told them what had happened and they went back again. Joan isn't going home for the funeral so she'll just remember Virg the way he was the last time she saw him. He's only 30 and Joan 26. Pretty young to be left alone and then have T.B. on top of it. She cried and cried all last night but I tried my best to comfort her and did what little I could. Mrs. Oseth told me I should try and keep her mind occupied by talking so we did & she got to feeling better. But when I leave the room she's sobbing again when I get back so am going to stay with her all the time so she doesn't have to be alone. When her folks came here after she first knew, I stayed down with Ardis Bilben several hours so they could talk alone but Joan asked Mrs. Reed if I could come back because she wanted me with her when they left. It made me feel good to think I could help her in some little way like that. This morning she's much better and we've been talking a lot. It seems that the only solution to keeping her mind away from thinking so much – those quiet hours at night when everything is dark is what's bad. We took up a collection for a memorial and got $13.75. When the nurse handed the sympathy card with it to her it opened up the wound again and she of course broke down. But I will say this – she's very brave about everything and I know she'll be okay. It will take time like all things. And say, Mom, don't worry about this being *hard on me because, as Mrs. Reed, our charge nurse, said, "Marilyn's a strong girl" (ha!) and, after all, I'm almost grown up – eighteen, you know. I know Joanie needs someone to stick by her and I'm the one to do it so I'm going to help her all I can.*

SATURDAY [OCTOBER 6]

I'm pretty sure they're going to let me come home. Dr. Callahan just made rounds and he said he'd look at the x-ray I had yesterday and my charts to see if everything is okay. Gee, I hope so cuz I want to come home while the leaves and trees are so beautiful. We're having just lovely weather now and today they took Joan out for a wheelchair ride. I know it will do her a world of good. She's very brave, tho'. If everything is okay, I'd like to come home as soon as possible, maybe next week. Have you seen Dr. Larson about the appointment? Dr. Callahan said he'd write you right away as soon as he knew.

OCTOBER 8, 1945 [MONDAY]

Joan's mother & Dad were here on Wednesday and then were up again on Saturday. Joey was along, too, so they had a nice visit. He is such a darling little boy – it's wonderful that Joanie has him to be of comfort to her. She's taking everything in stride and I know the worst is over now. She seems much more happy and takes interest in things. Boy, did I rate Saturday! Got letters from both Ralph and Earl Bemis. They are two swell fellas. Also was down to visit Elmer. He seems to like me kinda well cuz he asked me to come down there as often as I could to see him. My, my! What fun it is to be the center of so much attention! (I hope you don't think I'm getting conceited, tho.) Everything is so perfectly wonderful now at "Ching." I feel like I'm on top of the world today. Mrs. Reed, our charge, is wonderful and her husband, who's the janitor, couldn't be nicer. Today I love everybody. In fact I could just squeeze 'em. That's cuz I'm so happy about coming home, I guess. Dr. Callahan hasn't been around yet but suppose when he does come he'll tell me what he decided about my trip. I would like to come home as soon as possible. Wish Doc Cal would make rounds so I could find out. If it's pretty cold I can wear that tan winter coat of mine with the fascinator and white mittens I made myself. Those new grey slacks sure will come in handy. I won't be going places much so don't have to worry about clothes. Besides I want to wait til I'm all well before I go spending a lot of money on such things. I know Dr. Callahan will write you about this in time but I might as well tell you now. Dr. Kinsella thinks I should have a thorocoplasty this winter so I'm all prepared for surgery again. When Crow told me I wasn't very surprised because I was expecting it all along. Haven't asked them much about it as yet and I'm certainly not worried because I know it is the best thing and if I can have it soon I'll be home before next Christmas (1946). It seems like a long time off but really it isn't when you're used to terms of months and years instead of "weeks" like we are up here. I haven't asked about the culture yet but s'pose it was positive. I know everything will be fine, and I'm so thankful to have such a wonderful surgeon as Kinsella. We can talk this all over when we get together – and I hope that'll be very soon.

▪ Marilyn had seen other patients undergo the surgery, which involved removing ribs to collapse the lung, and have positive outcomes. She said it was a joy to watch others go home after the procedure, and she hoped for the same for herself.

TUESDAY MORN. [OCTOBER 9]

Dr. Callahan finally made rounds last night at supper time and said he had seen my x-rays. He said, "Your plate looks good" and that I can go home. I can go anytime you come up and get me, Daddy, and I'm pretty sure I can stay 2 weeks cuz everyone that goes home on vacation stays that long. It probably will take quite a few appointments to get the dental work done, too, and oh say, tell doctor I'd like to get the work done preferably in the morning or if I can't then in the afternoon after 2:30 cuz I have to take my rest hours and I'm going to be strict about them.

▪ While Marilyn had her two-week vacation at home, she went to her regular dentist, Dr. Larson. He told her it looked like someone had thrown acid in her mouth, and then he pulled a couple of teeth and put fillings in others.

SATURDAY [OCTOBER 27]

I hope you got home early and safe and sound last night. I'm already getting used to the quiet and one thing – I sure have plenty to keep me busy. This morning I'm just going to write letters and this afternoon if we don't have visitors I'm going to read the stories in my Ladies Home Journal. Thanks for making everything so swell while I was home.

MONDAY [OCTOBER 29]

Joan's folks were here and they had a nice visit. They had been to Itasca before coming here. Yesterday morning Ralph's dad was down to visit and he brought me a box of chocolates & some bananas. Don't know whether the candy was from him or Ralph but it was nice of him anyway. Wed. night I'm going to a Halloween party up on BIII. Lucy N. & Lucy C. and I are giving it. I'm going to buy the ice cream with the money Nita gave me. Gee, I'll have fun making the jack o'lantern. Hope we have a good time up there. I'm getting used to the place slow but sure. It really seemed different when I came back.

NOVEMBER 1ST [THURSDAY]

I'm sorry I didn't get a letter off to you yesterday but everything was in such a dither, going downstairs for aspiration and everything. By the way, he couldn't get in so he thinks my space is closed. In other words: my fluid is gone. He's going to try to find the space in about three weeks again just to be sure. Say, thanks so much, Mom and everyone, for the swell Halloween cookies, candy, nuts, and stuff. We sure had a successful party last night. I went up to Lucy's alcove at 7 (with my little pass in hand) and stayed til 9 o'clock when <u>dear</u> Mrs. Weiber (the nite snoop) came to take me home. We had all the lights out with just the jack o'lantern lit. They always have so much fun on BIII. Sorta wish I was up there because down here it's just like *a graveyard since we have to be quiet for the surgery patients. And lately the nurses kick all the patients off the floor when they come visiting without passes. They sure are strict.*

NOV. 3, 1945 [SATURDAY]
Just think only 8 weeks until Christmas—and me with no presents in the making. Harriet is going to let me have a quilted blue bed jacket of hers cuz she has so many but I'm going to give her something for it. Sure will come in handy during these cold months. Joan got her quilt down the other day so now we both have our "heavies" on.

MONDAY – NOVEMBER 5TH
Well, folks, Dr. Callahan made rounds on Saturday and he asked me if you had decided yet about "getting me fixed up" so I can get back to St. Peter soon. I told him I tho't you (Mom & Dad) would sign it and said that that was the only thing holding it up. Maybe if you write him they'll send you the papers to sign. I'm sort of anxious to get it over with, but just the same wish some new wonder drug would come out for T.B. and I wouldn't have to have it. Wish we could find out more about those drugs that have been in the papers – and when they'll be ready for public use.

■ Marilyn's mother was against her having the surgery. Marilyn had seen what other women looked like afterward, with scars and a concave chest, but she wanted protection against the TB reactivating. Marilyn begged her mother to sign the papers and explained that she didn't care about the deformity if she could live a normal life.

* * *

I sure have been disgusted lately cuz I haven't been getting mail from anyone else but you folks. Maybe I should write a few letters but golly I don't owe many. And when I was home they all told me to be sure and write!!
[LATER:]
In the bathroom this morning I weighed 132½ so I'm gettin' there. I'll have

to have some extra pounds in case I lose from surgery. They usually lose from 5 to 10 lbs. Fanchon Fischer has been quite sick lately, and today she had a special x-ray. Gosh, she was getting along so good – I sure hope she isn't getting a spread so she can't have surgery this winter.

p.s. Am enclosing a picture of "Pal", our pet fawn, for Keith.

■ Pal was an orphan fawn found by a farmer and brought to Ah-gwah-ching by a game warden. She was bottle-fed by the sanatorium steward's children, Bobby and Jeralyn, and stayed in their

Pal, the tame fawn

yard until she was big enough to jump the fence. During hunting season, Pal wore a red jacket made from a blanket. The photo was tinted by Al Strom.

THURSDAY [NOVEMBER 8]

Joan got a new blanket for winter and it's just like mine so our beds match. We have blouse alike and slacks alike, too. Speaking of clothes, yesterday Harriet sent down her blue satin quilted bed jacket and it's just darling. It has a few spots on it so she told me to use the money I'd give her for the dry cleaning bill. They have a regular dry cleaning service from Brainerd up here so think I'll send it out. The color of the bed jacket is baby blue and it sure looks nice on me.

NOVEMBER 13, 1945 [TUESDAY]

Mom and Daddy,

I talked with Dr. Callahan yesterday and told him that you folks would sign the papers for my surgery. He said that they'd be sent to you as soon as possible and he was pretty sure then that I'd have my first stage the next *surgery schedule. Gee, I sure was glad to hear that I could get it in so quick. Mom, I know what you'll say now – that this will spoil my Xmas and everything, but really, I don't mind one Xmas when this way I'll be home for good next Xmas. I'm really tickled that I can get to have it so soon cuz then by spring I'll be up on privileges again. Some times when I lie awake I practically fight with myself trying to think and decide which is best to do. But I know that in the end, surgery is what I really want. I know that if I didn't have it, I'd live in constant fear of breaking down and having to come back on the cure because as they say – my cavity would not hold up. Dr. Callahan made me feel very good when he went out the door yesterday. He said that I'm in wonderful condition so have nothing to worry about. And when he talked to me before, he said that I could lead a normal life afterward, have children and everything. Of course, there will be some restrictions, just as anyone who has had T.B. will have. Yes, I would like one of you to come up here to be with me when I have the 1st stage. It sure will help a lot cuz, well, this is the 1st major operation I've had. I'm not afraid but I'd just feel better if one of you were here for a few days. I'll probably have a roommate (either Lucille Stallman or Solveig Ohman – both packs) and we'll have a Christmas tree and everything. Just think – at this time next year, I'll be home with you all again. That's what I'm going to keep thinking all through surgery.*

▓ Lucille and Solveig had cavities reopen after thoracoplasties, so Dr. Kinsella inserted a pack—small pieces of paraffin—to add pressure. Paraffin was used because it could be molded to fill the cavity. It usually involved additional surgery to remove it after a collapse was achieved.

* * *

Gee, I sure hope you can find me another pair of rayon or cotton pajamas cuz I'll need quite a few for changes during surgery and won't be able to send them to the laundry. I wish the aunts and uncles would write me when I have surgery. I haven't heard from any of them (except Nita of course) for over 2 months. You can have the job of writing to them about my operation,

Mom. I hope they won't expect me to write for about 3 mos. Cuz it'll be over a period of almost 2 months that I'll be having my 3 stages.

P.S. I'm going to save a couple of ribs for souvenirs. Ha!

NOVEMBER 15 [THURSDAY]

I talked with Dr. Crow today and he said it's pretty sure I'll have my first surgery on Dec. 6th or 7th. Just after I'd written you the other day that I hadn't heard from any of the relatives, I got a card from Auntie Ruth and a box full of gum and Lifesavers from Uncle Gerold.

NOVEMBER 17 [FRIDAY]

I had my exam yesterday but didn't find out anything that I didn't already know. My x-ray looked real good – especially the right side – had no marks at all and Dr. Crow said I won't have to worry about that ever breaking down after I get my left side collapsed. He said my blood should be up a little so is giving me some iron tablets. Otherwise, everything is just fine – my weight, blood pressure, sedimentation, etc.

MONDAY [NOVEMBER 19]

Yesterday was such a quiet Sunday. I finished reading "Macbeth" and that's all I got done.

WEDNESDAY [NOVEMBER 21]

Dr. Crow did get into the space today but there were just a few teaspoonfuls of fluid. He said that after the collapse it will dry up completely. I'm going to be the only one having surgery now for a while. Don Moen & Elmer Nistler are both having their packs taken out this next time so will be right next door to them. And also Leonard Olson from upstairs is having his first stage then, too. Yesterday Joan had her exam and she got her first privilege. Boy, was she thrilled! We walked to the bathroom together for the first time this morn. Everyone tells me I'm so lucky to get in so soon because so many have had to wait 'til spring. I'm also thankful to have Dr. Kinsella – he's swell. Every day I pray to God and I know he'll bring me through this fine so I'm not worrying a bit. I hope you folks won't either. After all, surgery isn't the worst thing to go through and it's what's going to make me well and get me home.

NOVEMBER 22 [THURSDAY]
Happy Thanksgiving! Gee, gosh 'n' golly, we are having a regular wintry blizzard and the old north wind is blowing and howling around the corner of the buildings. We're sure lucky to be on the south side of the C building. From what we hear, they're really preparing a feast for us today. 60 turkeys and that's a lot of turkey! We've been having the most terrible meals up until today – baloney and wieners for 4 days straight. I guess they were trying to starve us so we'd eat good today. I hope you all have a nice Thanksgiving, too. We certainly have a lot to be thankful for.

SATURDAY MORN, NOVEMBER 24TH
Now-a-days hardly any visitors come around cuz they've been clamping down on so much running around. Dr. Leggett (the woman doctor) is the one who has started it and now even if the patients ask for passes they won't give them any. I guess some of the kids forged them or sumpin'. So- - - now I really get a lot more done since no one comes to visit.
P.S. How about sending me some Christmas T.B. seals?

Dr. Elizabeth Leggett had developed pleurisy after graduation from medical school and "took the cure" in California. Her strictness may have evolved from her personal knowledge of how patients behave.

MONDAY [NOVEMBER 26]
There certainly isn't much to write about today cuz we spent a very quiet weekend. Joan's folks brought us all kinds of good stuff from their Thanksgiving dinner – fruit cake, cold turkey and dressing, fresh rolls, pickles, and

I got my first taste of "lefsa." I really liked it too – all rolled up with butter and pieces of turkey inside. Guess they're turning me into a real <u>Norwegian</u>!

WEDNESDAY [NOVEMBER 28]
Thanks so much for the Christmas seals and letter, Mom. Tomorrow, Joan and I are going to the show, "Hollywood Canteen." Will maybe be dressed alike in our green blouses and grey slacks. I got the green blouse, Mom, and really the color looks lovely on me. Remember? My hair is turning more reddish!

16. SURGERY AND RECOVERY

Please don't worry now

DECEMBER 3, 1945 [MONDAY]

As far as I know, my first operation will be on Thursday. Wow! Did Kittleson ever give me the works! He took blood out of my arm to test for hemoglobin and blood count, clotting time, and type. Then he stuck the end of my finger for bleeding time. It really was interesting to watch him do all those tests. Afterwards he let me go into the lab room and I looked through his microscope at the different types of blood. I asked him who gives blood if we need transfusions, and he said either some of the employees or the prisoner boys at the farm. They're all typed so are just called if needed. Elmer Nistler had to have a transfusion cuz he had a pack put in after his 3 stages of thoracoplasty and he got blood from some prisoners. Boy, do they kid him about it cuz that "con" did something kinda awful. Everything's all set now. We have a new bunch of nurses again this morning and they all are efficient and well liked. Miss Porter especially. She's had T.B. herself and Joan said she knows just how to fix you up comfortable and everything. Mrs. Abrahamson is very good, too. Of course, for the first 4 days we have a "special" for both night and day. Mrs. Madison [Mattison] is day nurse and you couldn't find a more perfect nurse. She's just wonderful and I've talked with her a lot. Miss Jones, the white-haired lady, is on nights, and I think she's good, too. We've had her before so I know her well. How long can you stay, Daddy? I wish you could stay over until Sunday and then take the 1:24 p.m. bus home cuz they usually don't get to feeling better til Sunday. Even though I won't be able to talk very much it will make me feel so much better just to have you in the room. Please don't worry now, all of you, because everything will go just fine. I'm not a bit afraid although I'm not expecting it to be a "snap" cuz it surely won't be. But it helps you a lot to think that others have gone through it so I surely can, too.

DECEMBER 5, 1945 [THURSDAY]
I just had my special bath for surgery so now I'll write this letter to you. I s'pose by the time you read this tomorrow I will be down in the operating room almost halfway through my first stage. Sometimes they change things at the last minute, but as far as they know now – I'm to be the first one tomorrow at 8:30. I'm so glad I can be first cuz right after I wake up in the morning they'll dope me up and I won't know or feel a thing until it's all over. Most all the patients stay awake during the surgery but Don Moen & Elmer said they were so doped and slap-happy they didn't care what happened. Mrs. Reed, our charge, gave me permission to go up to visit Ralph

Nurses

yesterday afternoon and I had such a good time. He & his roommate were swell and it sure made me feel good the way they talked. Then I went next door to see Leonard – he's having his 1st stage tomorrow right after mine. Oh Mom, everyone I saw up there wished me the best luck and were so nice. I have so many "real" friends in this place. I'll really miss them terribly when I go home. Everything's all set. I get an enema and Mrs. Reed will shave my back this afternoon. Oh, what fun!

■ Before surgery, Marilyn was given Demerol to relax her and make her feel sleepy. Then she had a shot of Novocain to deaden the layers of skin. Dr. Kinsella used a scalpel to slit open the covering over her rib and snipped out part of it, leaving enough to regenerate. Marilyn was awake enough to hear the cutting of flesh and clipping of ribs, which she described as "a terrible sound." However, she was drowsy enough not to care and did not feel pain. The incision on her back was closed with twenty-six stitches. She was not allowed to drink fluids immediately after surgery but had a wet washcloth applied to her lips and mouth. Her first food was tea and toast. Her first real meal was, unfortunately, spareribs.

MON. AFT. [DECEMBER 10]
I'm really feeling swell this afternoon so will get a card off to you. Sorry I felt so rotten the 4 days Daddy was here and couldn't visit much. This morning Dr. Crow took out my stitches. Healed just swell – no drainage at all cuz I was in such "wonderful condition." I'll feel better every day from now on. I sit up by myself, eat and wash, and can move my left arm fairly good. It still is plenty sore. So is my back. This surgery really wasn't bad at all.

[UNDATED, PROBABLY WEDNESDAY, DECEMBER 12]
Today maybe I can get this letter off to you cuz I'm feeling really good. Yesterday was bothered with such a miserable stomach and didn't hardly eat a thing. The awful meals we've been having haven't helped either. Oh, how I long to have some nice crisp salads and spicy hot dishes! Everything

is so flat and soupy here – no wonder I have no appetite. Last night tho' I had some of those whole tomatoes and they shore did hit the spot! Today I'll have some of the ice cream. Have been very saving on the things Dad brought up cuz they taste so good and I hate to go back to the "plain" diet. It seems that for about 2 weeks before each holiday Lena, the dietician, thinks she has to starve us so we live on baloney, mutton (phew!) and such stuff. Joanie comes over every evening with the paper. Otherwise haven't had any other visitors cuz the "No Visitors" sign is still tacked on the door. I do get very lonesome for someone to talk with once in a while. Maybe I'll have a roommate for the holidays. Elmer & Don are so darned full of fun even though they're in more pain than me. We're all pretty sore yet but we'd laugh and then in unison say, "Ohh, Ohh!" and then laugh again even if it did hurt. The tight binders help a lot, though.

◼ The binders served two purposes: one was to protect the area of surgery and the regenerating ribs, the other was to keep the chest compressed so that the regenerating ribs would not follow their normal course but would be flattened to keep the lung deflated. Marilyn's binder was made of double fabric and was fastened with big safety pins down the front. She had to lie on her back and also have sandbags on her chest. Together, they pressed down on the new ribs as they regenerated. The new ribs formed a hard chest wall in that collapsed position. Once her surgeries were complete, Marilyn never again breathed with her left lung. Her upper chest was slightly concave, and she always wore padding on that side of her brassiere.

FRIDAY [DECEMBER 14]

I spent a very restless night but feel good today anyway. I'm off all hypos now and it sure seems funny. This morning when they looked at my back they said it sure looked good. I'm not as sore now either and everyone marvels at the way I get around and how good I look. My face is just as fat and they say I look like I didn't ever have 4 ribs out.

▓ Olga Hultberg wrote to Marilyn's parents on the fourteenth: "Just a line to let you know I have been down to see your darling daughter and she is feeling swell and amazes me how strong she is! She looks the same as always and with that cheery disposition and contagious laughter she'll go sailing through her surgeries. It would be nice if we all could be like her."

MONDAY MORNING [DECEMBER 17]

Well, this morning I sure feel swell! This morning I think we all go downstairs for x-rays and blood tests so we're going to stop in to see each other if the nurse will let us. I think I'll be able to go in a wheelchair and maybe will get up to sit on a chair while my bed's being made – if Crow says so.

WEDNESDAY [DECEMBER 19]

Well, I suppose Mom has already boarded the ol' bus for Ching by now, as it's 7:30 and I'm listening to Dayton's program. Gee, hasn't it been chilly, tho'? I hope Mom won't freeze up in this country. Last night we watched the eclipse of the moon – did you? I've gotten so much mail the past few day – on Monday got only 23 letters – or rather Xmas cards, but almost every one had a letter in it. So far, I have gotten many packages but then I've opened 3 already. Hmmm, such a bad gal! Sure wish I could see you all for Christmas, but we'll just have to be contented to wait for next year. The year 1946 holds much happiness for us, I'm sure.

▓ Marilyn's mother was with her for the second stage of surgery. It was in approximately the same area of her back and removed more rib ends.

DEC. 27TH [THURSDAY]

This won't be very long – just enough to let you know that I'm feeling pretty good. Still stiff and sore, but I really enjoy life more now and am eating lots better. In another week, I'll be through with my last stage. Goody! I don't think anyone will have to come up for it as it won't be bad – they tell me. Thank you all so much for the lovely Xmas presents.

SATURDAY [DECEMBER 29]

Well, it's snowing again this morning. Gosh, it's been cold & does my new flannel night shirt feel good. Wore it for the first time last nite. Lucille and I are having a grand time together and both are feeling swell again now. Crow did dressings yesterday & when I asked him about my next stage he said I wasn't going to have it next week because they have to start a couple of new surgeries. Darn! And I wanted to get it over with so soon. Lucille can't be on the list this next time either, because her blood is down and she felt bad about that, too. But then, we'll have fun together and the next 3 weeks will go fast.

JANUARY 1ST, 1946, NEW YEAR'S DAY

Happy New Year!! Boy, I'm glad that old 1945 is in the past and this new year has started that will bring me home. We all spent a very quiet New Year's Eve as the staff said, "no open house" because the patients acted so awful on Christmas. Gosh, you could have heard a pin drop on CII last night – honest. This morning I get a bath and then they move me back to my old room cuz I'm not having surgery this week. Yesterday Dr. Crow said he hadn't seen my X-ray yet (I had it taken yesterday morning and went in a wheelchair) so they don't know for sure yet if I'll even need a 3rd stage. He said maybe 2 would be enough but I'm counting on the 3rd because they've told so many that. He said there was "no special hurry" but golly I think so.

[LATER:]

Now I'm all moved back with Joanie again and it certainly seems good although this room seems terribly tiny compared to our nice big room next door. We're having a big turkey dinner with all the fixin's in about half an hour. Yum-yummy! I'll really enjoy this one lots more than on Christmas Day a week ago. This afternoon we will probably just take it easy and listen to the Elgin program with all the movie stars, etc.

▪ Elgin's *Two Hours of Stars* shows, sponsored by the Illinois-based Elgin Watch Company, started in 1942 especially for the soldiers overseas, and the holiday specials featured stars from radio and the movies. Marilyn also enclosed a list of the people from whom she received gifts and what they gave—twenty-nine presents in all. Her mother wrote the thank-you notes for her.

JAN. 2, 1946, LATE AFTERNOON [WEDNESDAY]

Oh, this has been a quiet day at Ching but, boy, it seems good to be back in the old place again. My bed here is soft, but gosh, it's hard to get used to after that hard one that rolled up & down. Here is some news that will probably surprise you. John O'Donnell passed away a few days ago.

SATURDAY [JANUARY 5]

Boy, has this weather ever been awful! By the way, I'm having my 3rd stage in 2 weeks. Kinsella stopped in Thursday nite to see me and I had him autograph my rib. Gee, he's nice. He said they decided to clip off a few more ends of the top ribs in front just to make sure. So this stage will be just the finishing up and won't be bad. I don't think anyone will have to come for it. Boy, I'll be glad to be through! Although I didn't think this surgery was so bad and everyone including the doctors think it was so remarkable how fast I picked up after each stage. I haven't lost much weight or anyway have gained it back already. People tell me I don't look like I'd gone through anything at all. I feel super!

   ▨ Marilyn's New Year's resolution, as printed in *The Moccasin*: "To refrain from discussing my operation more than ten times a day and showing my pet 'rib' to everyone who comes in."

WEDNESDAY [JANUARY 9]

How's every little thing down that-a-way? Every thing's swell up here except that about everyone who works in this place is coughing, sneezing or has the flu. Dr. Callahan is in a Mpls. Hospital with it, so we're sure worried about him. He's had T.B., too, you know. I'm really getting limbered up now with all the exercises for my arm, etc.

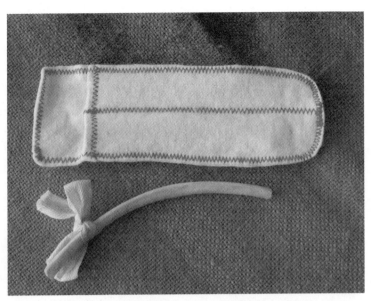

One of Marilyn's ribs removed during surgery

■ There were no physical therapists at Ah-gwah-ching. Doctors told patients what exercises to do, and it was up to them to follow through. Marilyn knew it was important to regain the full movement of her arm and to avoid the tendency to let the shoulder droop, which could result in a permanent slouch of her left side. She extended her right arm and then stretched her left arm over and pretended to play piano, running the scales up and down her right arm from shoulder to wrist. Rose Soper sent Marilyn a get-well card and told her to "keep that arm a-movin'—advice from one who knows what it is all about."

* * *

Yesterday they told me I should start combing my own hair so Joanie helped me put it up in curlers. Looks fairly nice today although it's terribly dirty. Dr. Crow gave me permission to have a shampoo before my last stage.

JAN. 11TH, FRIDAY

On Wednesday, Dr. Crow tried for fluid and evidently my space is gone because he couldn't find a drop. Boy, I was glad! My incision is perfectly healed – not even any scabs left so don't have any dressings on or even a binder. Feel naked without it, tho! I still have the sand bag on and will have until a week or so after my 3rd stage. Hope to get a shampoo tomorrow cuz my head itches something awful.

MONDAY [JANUARY 14]

Oh, what a gorgeous morning! Little "Pal" just came across the snow to take his morning nap on the skylight of the tunnel where it's warm. I haven't heard the exact day for my surgery but I think it will be on Thurs. I'll be in the end room alone for the first few days as they have plenty of empty rooms, but after we get better Mrs. Reed said Lucille & I could be together. Dr. Callahan is back now and feeling okay. He made rounds and sure cheered me up. Said my last stage wouldn't be bad, and then I'd be all through. Fanchon is having her first stage on the 31st.

TUESDAY A.M. [JANUARY 15]

I'm having surgery day after tomorrow (Thursday) at 8 o'clock in the morning. I'm so glad to be first cuz then I just wake up and go right down and it'll be all over by 11 o'clock. This morning Don, Lucille, and I went down to the lab for blood tests & x-rays. Lucille has surgery right after me on Thursday. I hope we all get along okay. It's one of those cold clear days today, and I do mean cold! Last night and this morning it was 30° below!! Jeeps! And our pipes almost froze, too – not to mention us! Ha! I've got my binder back on – It feels so good. Saw Mabel and she said Elsie might go home this month.

JANUARY 16, 1946, WEDNESDAY MORN

Tomorrow at this time I'll probably be on my way down to the operating room. I'm not dreading it in the least cuz I know it won't be bad. Joan said she'd write and keep you posted until I'm able to write again. In a few minutes, Jo Golberg will be coming in to give me a bath. Boy, do I rate all the attention around here. Then this afternoon I get an enema. Ugh! That's one attention I'd rather not have!!!!

Postcards to the Barnes family from Joan

THURS. [JANUARY 17]

Hello folks!

Your little gal just came up from surgery and it's only ten minutes after ten. My, it must have gone slick! Since one always waits in the hall before they take you into the operating room, she must only have been in there an hour & some. Callahan & Kinsella were just in here & they said she is O.K. – everything went wonderful from the time she got on the table and all thro it. I'll be going in to see her every day after she gets to feeling better. So don't worry about your Marilyn! She's O.K. I'm so glad it's all over.

Love to all – Joan

FRI. MORN. [JANUARY 18]

Marilyn is doing just fine. She had such a good long rest between the 2nd & 3rd stages. I ask the nurses about her & the doc & they all tell me she feels & acts better this time than last. Honestly, I've never seen sleeping tablets work as fast on anyone – she'd get sleepy in less than 5 minutes. Quite a few of the gals have colds so I've almost been alone in the bathroom mornings. Bye now. Greet all. Love, Joan

SAT. MORN. [JANUARY 19]

I had Mrs. Madison [Mattison], special nurse, ask Marilyn if there was any special message for you folks this morning. She said to tell you the stage was the easiest of them all & that she is feeling great! I'm so happy for her. It's going to get her home soon now for good. I was rather expecting my folks up this weekend, but they won't be up. The boys had the car the other nite & a front wheel came off. Our poor car is on the road almost all day

*steady. Dad uses it from early morning till nite & then the boys use it to give
their gals a spin. Jim comes home weekends & Bill is home.*

By now – Love, Joan

Marilyn resumed her letters

WEDNESDAY, JAN. 23RD, 1946

*I'm feeling swell now – getting stronger and peppier every day so it shouldn't
be any time at all now until I'm back to normal. I kind of get a kick out of
the way you folks think I'll be home by June. I may be so "well" by June
but I <u>know</u> I won't be home by then so don't plan on it too hard. They'll
be giving me lots of walking exercise before I get a discharge and I figure
that <u>if</u> I get my first privilege in April or the 1st part of May I'll be able to
go home by Aug. or September. But <u>please</u> don't plan too hard on anything
cuz so many things can happen in this game. I've seen and heard so many
things that have happened to others – not that they are going to happen
to me! Joanie comes down every nite but I haven't been very lonesome in
the day time as Richard Morgan, the young Indian fellow across the hall,
talks to me all the time. He is so cute and what a witty guy. He's really half
Negro & half Sioux Indian so he's very dark, but such a handsome Negro.
When we both sit up, we can see each other and I love to watch him when
he laughs – his white teeth just flash! He lives in the Black Hills but went
2 yrs. to the U of M. Today they are moving him back to EIII, and I sure
will miss him. He said he's going to send over a dish of wild rice to me. It's
a favorite food of the Indians.*

    ■ The "Who's New" column in *The Moccasin* said Richard Mor-
gan's "generosity and friendliness is hard to equal." Richard was
from Rosebud, South Dakota. He was born in 1918 and attended
both Dunwoody Institute and the University of Minnesota. Before
entering Ah-gwah-ching he was an engineering aide for the War
Department. "Who's New" noted he was married and the father of
two healthy children, an important point to make for the offspring
of a tuberculous parent. The column said his favorite pastime was

reading, and he hoped to return to work as a civil servant. The nurses told Marilyn it was good that she and Richard were recovering at the same time because they had so much in common—Marilyn read a lot and Richard had been to college. At the time Marilyn thought the comment funny because there were no blacks or Native Americans in St. Peter and Richard was almost ten years older.

THURSDAY [JANUARY 24]
Not much news today except that Dr. Crow gave Joan a bathtub privilege! Wow, isn't that some news? She's still shaking with excitement. Gee, now that means she won't be with me much longer cuz when they get outdoor exercise they move to DII. Maybe Lucy Carlson on CIII and I can get together cuz her roommate Lucy N. will be moving to DII soon, too.

JANUARY 25, 1946, FRIDAY AFTERNOON
I'm starting this letter for tomorrow's mail early because I might get interrupted with a bath and moving back in the morning. Gee, I'm glad to be leaving this lonesome old room. I've had to fight to keep myself busy & occupied since Richard went. We sure had fun talking across the hall. I guess having the same disease binds people together since they have the same interests, etc. I've found that true even with us thoracoplasty patients and when we get together we have quite an enjoyable time comparing notes on our operations. Ha! Fanchon went down to the lab this morning for her surgery blood tests and x-ray. Boy, I know just how she feels cuz I did exactly the same thing 8 wks ago. Sure is a swell feeling to know you're through and I hope Fan gets along as good as I did. I haven't any idea when I'll be able to go to shows again, Mom, but at present I'm pretty contented to stay right in bed. I'll have to get a lot stronger and more used to sitting up for long periods before I'll dare to go cuz thorocoplasty patients get pretty tired at first since so many ribs are gone in the back. It doesn't ever bother tho' after the ribs are regenerated and the patient is used to exercise. My scar in front (from the 3rd stage) sure is a little one;

I mean – not very long. It makes a nice little half circle from underneath my armpit to under my breast. My breast is sunken in some, now, but that will get better in a few months. I don't think I'll show my scars or side to you folks until after I get home cuz, well, it isn't a very pretty sight to see. Then, too, by that time I will be more filled out. Gee, this sounds like it's really terrible, but if you've never seen a thoro before you might not like it. I'm not as sunken in as some, though. The other day I was asking someone how much the 3 operations would have cost if I had to pay for it and it comes to around $1,500 for the whole thing. Golly – just think if we would have had to pay for it ourselves. Whew!

17. ROOMMATES, ROMANCE REPEAT

You never know what's going to happen in this place

MONDAY MORN. [JANUARY 28]
It's sure swell to be back with Joanie again. We talked and talked – just like we'd been apart for months. She, of course, gets up to go to the b.r. quite a bit but it doesn't make me want to get up and run around cuz I'm very contented to stay in bed for a while. We had turkey dinner yesterday, and it wasn't a holiday either.

JAN. 29, 1946, EVENING [TUESDAY]
This morning I really got "the works." First of all I had an x-ray and blood test. Then I just got settled in bed when Crow called me downstairs for aspiration. He couldn't get any fluid so looks like it's left me for good. Yesterday Ruth Jones & Rose Soper moved to the wards. So tomorrow Joan & I are moving into Soper's room. Will seem kind of good to have a change of scenery after being in this room for over 2 yrs. Vera, Harriet, & Ardis Bilben will be our neighbors. It's right around from the bathroom, too, so Joanie won't have so far to walk. Fan is getting all ready for surgery Thursday. Her roommate will be a little 14 yr old girl who just came today from another San to have an extra pleural. Cute kid!

■ The young girl came from Deerwood Sanatorium near Brainerd. The smaller county sanatoriums that didn't have surgical facilities sent patients to Ah-gwah-ching, Nopeming, or Glen Lake for procedures.

JANUARY 31ST [THURSDAY]

Boy is it ever fun to have a change! Joan & I are just crazy about this room. Down here, Molly & Harriet & Vera are so close, and we have more visitors and see more people go by. Another thing – we get away from all the hubbub of surgery down that end of the hall. Yes, I did lose some weight but don't know the exact number as I haven't been weighed. I was down to 119½ when I had my shampoo before my 3rd stage. I'll gain it all back soon.

FEBRUARY 2ND, 1946, "GROUNDHOG DAY" [SATURDAY]

I guess the lil' groundhog is going to see his shadow today as the sky looks kinda pink on the horizon. But is it ever cold! Jo Golberg just said that her thermometer said 35° <u>below</u>! Eek! Mrs. Cowley, our night nurse, comes in every real cold night at 2 o'clock and turns on our radiator. Isn't that nice of her? "Heidy" you know that gooney guy on CIV who's supposed to have a crush on me might come down tonight. So I'll just have to look my best. Ha! Speaking of fellas, I got a real cute letter from Ralph day before yesterday and he's been feeling lots better. Gee, I do hope he can make the grade—but he's sure got a long way to go.

◾ Marilyn met "Heidy," Roland Heiderscheid, during one of her trips to the treatment rooms.

MONDAY MORN [FEBRUARY 4]

It's another grey day and looks like snow. Gee, this weather is getting monotonous. I'm getting quite bored with just lying around doing nothing but reading & writing letters. Wish I could start a little knitting again. But I'll have to wait a while before I can start, I suppose. At any rate, I'm going to ask Crow first before I do. I'm anxiously awaiting my exam, but Crow is awfully far behind in them so it probably won't be for some time.

FEBRUARY 6TH [WEDNESDAY]

We're having quite a blizzard so I don't know whether the trains are even running for mail, etc. On the radio this morning I heard that schools in

St. Peter are closed. Bet Keith is glad of that. The other morning I told Dr. Crow I was getting awfully bored and he said, "Well, we'll be kicking you out before long—like Joan here." Gee, I just about fell over because he usually never says stuff like that. My spirits were high for the rest of the day just from those few words. Last night I was so surprised to hear that Glenn Haglund is back here.

FEB. 9, 1946 [SATURDAY]

I suppose down home as it is up here – the blizzard is the main topic of the day. Every tree and bush was covered with ice and when the sun finally came out it was really a sight to see. Looking out towards the woods made you think it was a forest made of glass and the glitter just about blinded me. I guess we didn't get as much snow as some parts of the state but we have had the lowest temperatures. 20° - 30° below yesterday and today. Boy, I'm glad I can be inside! Carl Hawkinson (we call him "Hawkie" for short) got a pass to come down to see us last night. He is more fun than a circus and we especially like him cuz he brings us hot egg & Spam sandwiches. The boys up there tease the dickens out of him cuz he's so shy and never tells who he's going to see. He is a middle-aged man – married and has children – but he just loves to come to visit Joan & I, and we enjoy visiting with him, too. "Romeo" Heidersheid got a pass to come and see me today (I heard by way of the grapevine). Oh oh! He's really quite the goon!

FEBRUARY 11, 1946 [MONDAY]

Yesterday Joanie took her first tub bath and was she thrilled! She now is full privileged – can walk everywhere – to shows, church, x-ray, etc., so is off wheelchairs forever! In about 2 weeks she should be going to the dining room so I imagine she'll be moving to DII the 1st part of March. I don't know what I'm gonna do for a roommate. I like this room down here so well, too, that I'd hate being in an alcove in the B Building. Maybe today I'll be getting my new binder jacket with the buckles down front and my sponge put in. I'll have to wear the sponge under my arm for around 6 months.

▓ Although Marilyn no longer had to lie with sandbags on her chest, it would still be months before her ribs were fully regrown. The new binder had pockets in it for sponges, and when the binder was tightened, the sponges provided the pressure needed to shape her ribs into the concave position.

FEBRUARY 16, 1946. SATURDAY

I suppose you are anxiously waiting to hear how our Valentine's Day party turned out. Well, we sure had loads of fun. Molly, Olga & Carmie made up the guests. Carmie cooked coffee and the ice cream and cake sure went fast. The cake was just scrumptious, Mom – everyone said so. We kept our door shut while they were here as it was surgery day and we didn't want to make too much noise. Molly (that typical Irish wit) told some stories, as did Carmie, and we just roared. By the time the party broke up we all had tears running down our cheeks, we laughed so hard. Ralph sent me a darling sweetheart Valentine. So did Roland Heidersheid. Richard Morgan had another stage of thoro this week (his 6th). He doesn't have any ribs left on his one side – boy, is that extensive. Don Moen & Lucille had their packs taken out yesterday and Fan and another fellow from CII had their 2nd stage so the "butcher" had pretty good business this week. I really feel good now and my appetite is swell. In fact, I've been eating like a horse so should gain quite a bit when we get weighed the 1st of next month.

MONDAY MORN [FEBRUARY 18]

Yesterday, Joan's mother, dad, Bill, Jackie, and Joey came up. She walked over to the reception room with them and when she came back she tried on some new clothes they bought for her. Boy, my mouth was just drooling. One dress was a cheery wool jersey with buttons down the front and the other was a tailored aqua wool gabardine. Now I can hardly wait til I start "walking" around so I can get new clothes, too.

THURSDAY [FEBRUARY 21]

Today Miss Emig is coming (this afternoon) for my 1st art lesson. Next

Monday I'll start school lessons again. Dr. Crow put the okay on it. Yesterday I had a shampoo and since our room is right across from the bathroom I walked over. I feel so strong – almost like I could take a privilege. Fanchon is coming along fine, but I don't know when her next stage will be. She's had two already.

FEBRUARY 23 [SATURDAY]
I've been writing thank you letters and have also been catching up on my letters to the gals in St. Peter. This morning I think I'll study. Tomorrow I'll practice my drawing lesson for next Thursday. Miss Emig is starting me out on a commercial art course & is it fun. She furnishes me with most of the pencils, paper, etc.

MONDAY [FEBRUARY 25]
We spent a very quiet Sunday as usual. I read about 20 pages in Eng. Literature, read the paper and listened to the radio. Exciting, huh? I'm now reading parts of "Paradise Lost" by Milton and "Pilgrim's Progress" by Bunyan. I think they're very interesting and I'm getting to like the Eng. classics more & more.

FEBRUARY 28, 1946 [THURSDAY]
Miss Emig was here for my lesson this afternoon, and we enjoyed chatting with her so much. For next week's lesson I have to draw solid objects such as pyramid, blocks, etc. I'm glad you got some more material, Mom. Say, be sure that the pattern you get doesn't have a wide or low neckline cuz I can't very well wear those yet for a while until I fill out more. The V-neckline or round high necklines are okay.

SATURDAY [MARCH 2]
Joan hasn't heard when she'll be moving but I suppose it'll be in a week or so. The San sure is filling up now, since the mobile x-ray units are going.
   ▪ The legislature provided funding for the Department of Health

Display used in parades to advertise mobile health surveys

to launch an aggressive campaign to reduce tuberculosis in Minnesota. Mobile units traveled throughout the state, offering free chest x-rays to citizens. People with active, contagious tuberculosis were referred to the sanatoriums.

MONDAY MORNING [MARCH 4]

First of all – I still plan on moving to BII. Joan hasn't any idea as to exactly when she'll be moving, but thinks it'll be within the couple of weeks. Here's the reason I want to move . . . Well, if I'd stay here they had it all planned to put me in with Sally Jackson and oh, gosh that would be terrible. She's so sick and lifeless and fussy – been here 9 yrs. and she's so much older. They plan on moving a couple of Indian girls over to CII cuz the E Building is so filled, so I wouldn't be able to keep my room without a roommate. While I've been here, Joanie is the only <u>real</u> pal I've had cuz all the others are so much older and married women have such different interests than young girls.

Even Joan included. Sometimes if you happen to act a little silly or cut-up, they think it's just awful and rather childish! So you see what I have to put up with. Yesterday Bill Oseth and another boy and their girlfriends drove up so Joan went over to the reception room with them. Gosh, sure makes me wish I could be out having good times with the kids. I'm to feel like an old lady being stuck with the patients on CII. Mr. Ohman was just here visiting his wife. Solveig is going to have a pack next month. Mabel B. went by with her sister Lili, who was up visiting yesterday so they stopped in for a little. She has 3 priv. but she gets those pneumo reactions, fluid, etc. She sure has her ups and downs. Vivian Olson has a privilege now so we'll probably be walking outside together this summer. Mabel Jones is finishing those p.j.s for me that I started last summer. I think they will be nice. I'm glad you folks got yourself some new spring togs. Sure am anxious to see you at Easter.

WEDNESDAY [MARCH 6]

It's snowing real hard but I guess we'll have to go through a lot of these disappointments before Spring comes to stay. Think I'll study English and practice my drawing this morning.

MARCH 8TH [FRIDAY]

I got the box of clean p.j.s yesterday – thank you for everything, folks. That little St. Patrick's pin is cute, Nita. I'll be sure to wear him come March 17th. Thanks to you, Grams, for the candy bar. Yes, we heard Churchill speak. I liked him very much, didn't you?

Winston Churchill's speech in Fulton, Missouri, on March 5, 1946, contained the statement that is generally believed to mark the beginning of the Cold War: "From Stettin in the Baltic to Trieste in the Adriatic, an iron curtain has descended across the continent."

MONDAY [MARCH 11]

Gosh, it seems like the weeks have been just edging along so slow. That must be cuz I'm so restless seeing Joanie up all the time. Boy, it's plenty hard to stay in bed and be contented when you have a roommate that has full priv. In about a week she'll be moved, we think cuz starting tomorrow she goes to all three meals in the dining room. I now weigh 121. Don't want to get as fat again – just right the way I am.

MARCH 13, 1946

The Moccasin came out yesterday and I thought they were very good this time so bought quite a few. There is a cute poem in there: "Ode to Van Johnson," so I decided to write him a fan letter and send him a Moc with his poem. I've only seen him in one picture – "Thirty Seconds over Tokyo" but hubba, hubba!! . . . he's okay! Well, it looks like I'm not going to move after all. The main reason I wanted to get off this floor was because I don't like it here in the first place. The patients are too dull and never do anything interesting and Dr. Crow has become so, well, negligent. He's still okay, I guess, but lately they have been doing so much surgery, and he pays a lot of attention to you then – but afterward, pooey! You're practically forgotten. You can't blame him I suppose cuz he's so busy all the time. When he makes rounds he never says much or asks how your sputum, temp & pulse is, like the other doctors do, and he's positively terrible when it comes to building you up on exercise. I've seen that in Joan's case – he leaves everything up to the patient and when you ask him anything his answers are so indefinite. In the end, Mrs. Reed, our charge, is really the one who has the last word about things. She's a regular dictator and lots of times she goes above his authority and no nurse is supposed to do that. Joan had one privilege and then Crow made her take full privileges all in one jump. In other buildings they work up gradually on 1, 2, 3, 4, and full privileges so it sure seems dumb. All the patients remark about it, too.

MARCH 16, 1945

Sure, 'n' 'tis St. Patrick's Day! Well anyway it will be when you are reading this (I hope!) Yesterday we had the window wide open all day and that wonderful spring air just about had me drooling, no kidding! Lucky Joan to be able to go walking outside soon – but I'm just as satisfied that I'll be having nice June weather when I get out there. (Did you notice my green ink in honor of the occasion? As if you could miss it! I made the shamrock out of used 1¢ stamps saved from all my "Locals" sent through the mail.)

■ Marilyn decorated the corner of her stationery by cutting cancelled stamps into three shamrocks and attaching a small ribbon bow. Without John O'Donnell to deliver intra-sanatorium mail, the patients now had to put postage stamps on cards and have them go through the Ah-gwah-ching post office.

* * *

Yes, I am a little weaker since surgery but every day I can feel more strength coming back. As soon as I get a privilege that will help – also my shortness of breath will go away. I don't puff all the time – so it isn't noticeable. It's just when I walk a ways like when I get up for bed making, etc. Gee, it seems like I get a lot more done since Joan is out of the room so much. In the mornings I write letters and draw (In art now I'm drawing a spiral figure to show light & shadow and I have to shade it – more fun!) Then in the afternoon I read my English Literature and after supper I read the paper and listen to the news, etc. At seven I usually pick up my crocheting while listening to all the evening radio programs so you see I organize my time to get a little bit of everything done each day. The rest hours sure cut up the time, tho!
P.S. Fanchon had her pack put in on Thursday so she's a pretty sick gal.

MONDAY [MARCH 18]
There were quite a few visitors and we got a lot of enjoyment watching the children play with "Pal" outside our windows. She sure loves little children & they can do most anything to her. It's so cute to watch her lick their faces and she follows them right up if they back away. All I accomplished was to read two Sunday papers (Joan gets the St. Paul Pioneer Press besides our other) and last night I drew a few border designs for my art lesson. This weather makes me think about new summer clothes – oh, golly, I wish I'd get a privilege soon!

MARCH 20, 1946 [WEDNESDAY]

If Doc "Cal" (the big boss, as Crow calls him) comes around today, Joan may get her permission for outside exercise. I sure hope she can so she can enjoy a few of these wonderful days before we get a snowstorm or something. Most of the day I just sit here and dream about the time when I'll be walking out there. It's almost as much fun as the real thing. Joanie sure has her troubles! Now her Dad just wrote that Joey has very bad eyes – in fact his one eye's vision is practically nil. Another thing her Dad wrote about was that the people they rent their home from are afraid of her now when she's coming to live with them because she's had T.B. Doesn't that make a person just furious!!? That just shows how ignorant the public is. Dr. Crow said that the doctors would write out a paper signifying that Joan is perfectly well and discharged with consent. I think I'd like a paper like that, too, just in case someone is in doubt about me when I get home.

MARCH 22ND [FRIDAY]

Joanie was to go outside but Callahan has gone to the Cities again so she'll have to wait til next week now. Then I think she'll move over too. She got all her clothes from home the other day so is rarin' to go. I was just drooling over the darling new pumps she got. Mmm! Yesterday afternoon Miss Emig came and, oh, she was so pleased with my first sketching. She said it deserved a "100" and I was as thrilled as a little school kid. Honest. Fan is feeling pretty rotten. Did you know Rose Soper was discharged and is home in Kato now?

MARCH 23RD [SATURDAY]

Measured my waist and it's 27½ only I think 28 in. would be better because you spread out more in this "bed position." Hope you can send the new pajamas back with the laundered ones.

MONDAY [MARCH 25]

Mrs. Ost passed away Saturday afternoon. It was so sudden, although we knew she had been failing for quite a while. Lou Ann, an uncle & younger sister were just here to get her things and the two girls stopped in. They were so brave – such swell kids and I felt so sorry for them. I imagine the younger ones will live with aunts & uncles.

▣ Minnie Ost's husband, Albert, had died in 1938. Minnie's six children ranged in age from ten to twenty.

MONDAY EVE. MARCH 25, 1946

So many things have been happening and I feel I've just got to talk with you. First of all, Doc Crow came in this afternoon and said they thought of putting me with Miriam Apitz on BII, but since they are crowded in the B Building, she will move down with me. Her dad has been here over the weekend and he talked with Callahan and wanted to know what was what and if Miriam couldn't have a suitable roommate he wanted to take her home. Well, Callahan got busy and he knew that I'd be alone now since Joan is moving so he thought Miriam and I would make good pals. Miriam and her dad walked by this afternoon from the reception room and she stopped to introduce him to me. Gee, I'm sure we'll get along super. She is quite short, blond, blue-eyed, and the thing that strikes you first is her friendliness. She belongs to the German Lutheran church I think. If we get together we'll sure have a lot of visitors and fun cuz there's never a dull moment for the "Moc" editor. Will continue tomorrow and give you the up-to-the-minute details after things get moving. G'nite now–

WEDNESDAY MORNING

Joanie moved to DII yesterday but so far they haven't done anything with me. I kind of think that Miriam will come down here today or tomorrow but you never know what's going to happen in this place. Dr. Crow said he'd find out and let me know today but he's busy giving pneumo this morning so I doubt whether he'll remember. Such a forgetful man! Last night, Tess Paulson had a "farewell" party for Joan. She came over from the wards and I got permission from Crow so I was down there, too. Hawkie and Art happened to come by so they just crashed the party. Sure was a lot of fun to get out and I surprised myself by not getting a bit tired. I sure slept sound all night, tho. It seemed so funny without Joan in the room at first but I'm not a bit lonesome. This morning I've got a lot of things to do (for one thing I've decided to write Heidersheid a letter telling him to stop coming down to see me & will that be a chore!)

▓ Roland was trying too hard to become Marilyn's friend and had become a bit of a pest.

MARCH 29, 1946, FRIDAY MORN

Yesterday it was really warm and we had the windows open until late at night. It was just like summer – the temperature was near 80° in the afternoon. Joan didn't come over to see me yesterday and was I lonesome. She had a metabolism test taken in the morning and she went to show in the afternoon and Lenten services at night so I can see she must have been pretty tuckered out. Yesterday Miss Emig came for my art lesson and gave me another plaster model to sketch. She wants me to learn the human anatomy I guess, for dress designing, etc. Ardi Bilben was so thrilled the other day over getting a "knitting privilege" (she's had heart trouble and has been pretty sick so Doctor Crow wouldn't let her do fancywork before this) that she treated all the girls on CII to Cheerios (ice cream bars on a stick).

▓ Good Humor's original ice cream bar on a stick sold for ten cents. When Popsicle came out with a five-cent ice bar, Good Humor introduced the Cheerio, a smaller five-cent version of its Good Humor bar, in 1931.

* * *

About 8 o'clock all the doctors, Kinsella, Callahan, Crow, and Black – came to see the surgery patients so they stopped in here. I'm so crazy about that man – Kinsella – he's a great kidder and what personality!! He asked me how my arm was and felt of my shoulder to see if it was staying down. Callahan stood and talked with me a while after they left, and he said that Crow & Black would get together to see about moving Miriam &

I together. "Of course", he said, "you'll be going to the wards before very long. Yes, Miss Barnes (he always calls me that) you'll be doing schoolwork back in St. Peter again this Fall." Boy, is he encouraging! It will seem so wonderful to be able to go to school again even though I will be with kids a few years younger. Just think – Keith & I will both be in High School – he a Freshie and me a Senior. Won't that be fun??

18. PROGRESS AND SADNESS

It's hard to be patient

MONDAY MORNING, APRIL FOOL'S DAY [APRIL 1]

*Saturday afternoon I had some patients in here all the time and that night
Earl Bemis came down for about an hour. He came to say goodbye cuz he
left yesterday for a few weeks at home and then will transfer to Glen Lake.
He is such a swell guy and I'll miss him a lot but he's going to write so we'll
at least keep in touch. He expects to have surgery sometime in the future so
he'll still be "on the cure" for some time. Maybe after I get discharged and go
to Mpls. I can stop out to visit at Glen Lake. Last night at a quarter to six I
had another visitor. You guessed it – another male! Marshall Lee Bex, that
boy from Walker who was here for fluid about 2 yrs ago. He hadn't stopped
in to visit for quite a while as he's been out in California working and just got
back. Oh, that cute guy! We talked and talked about everything from religion
to perfumes for 2 hours straight and some pretty hot discussions at that. (I
must take after Dad cuz I love to argue.) He sat on the empty bed across from
me (one advantage of being without a roommate. Ha!) and told me all about
the movie stars in Hollywood and the rooming house he lived in where there
were all kinds of characters – actors, musicians, poets, etc. Out West he said
that everyone is for Russia, and communism is getting terrible. Bex is 1A now
but he and a lot of the young fellows his age don't care to fight for this country
and be in its armed services because they don't like the way things are run.*

TUESDAY [APRIL 2]

*Well, I guess I won't be getting a roommate for a while now cuz Miriam is
going to start taking streptomycin shots and if they don't start those treat-*

ments here she will be transferred to Cannon Falls San. In a week or so, they'll know, so if she can take them here then we'll be roommates.

▨ Streptomycin, hailed as a miracle drug, successfully cured a young woman of TB in 1945. It was expensive, had several side effects including deafness, and needed to be administered under strict supervision. It wasn't obtained for patient use at Ah-gwah-ching until April 1947.

TUESDAY EVENING [APRIL 2]

Do I have good news for you! Yes, I had my long-awaited-for exam this morning. Dr. Crow showed me all the x-rays (the ones between stages, too) and I have a wonderful collapse. Sure looked funny, though, to see those ribs gone. My sputum has stayed negative since my culture, and I'll have another culture started soon. I asked about my blood, and he laughed and said, "Oh, it's good, red blood in the 90's." (anything between 80 and 100 is normal). So everything is on the up and up. He said I'll be up on exercise in a couple of months, and gosh, I just about fell over. So I should be getting my 1st privilege in April sometime and that will be followed up by the others and walking exercise. Gee, maybe I'll be home by July after all!

APRIL 4TH [THURSDAY]

This is the day I go to the show, "State Fair." Whoopee!! Yes, Dr. Crow gave me permission yesterday. Joanie is going to save a good seat for me. No, Mom, we didn't hear the Winter Carnival broadcast Saturday as Roland Heidersheid and Harold Edman were here visiting.

FRIDAY EVENING, APRIL 5, 1946

I've just finished supper and was anxious to have a "talk" with someone so might as well have one with you. Lot of the gals who go to the b.r. stop in during the day – especially Mabel and Molly, but I do get lonesome for someone to talk with in-between times. Next week is surgery again so I think they'll move Lucille in with me because she's through now and they *have to make room. When Fan finishes her pack in a month or so, she and Lucille will be roommates on this floor, I guess. At 12 noon yesterday, Ralph passed away. I was awfully surprised when Art Sabatke came down after church last night and told me. I'm sure thankful he did tell me, though, because I was thinking about Ralph all day and started a letter to him last night. It was really a blessing he did go – poor kid. He was only 22 yrs old. I feel very sorry for his dad because, as you know – Ralph's mother died of T.B. many years ago. It is nice that he has his second wife and baby son to comfort him, tho. Doesn't it seem that I have a jinx on all the boys up here who write to me? Benny & Ralph – both such swell boys, too. I guess I won't have any more so-called crushes while I'm up here – will wait til I get home and can pick some good healthy fella – huh, Mom? Now that Bemis and the rest are gone, I can't look for "locals" anymore. Joanie comes over every night to pass out our mail after supper so she was just in and got a couple of my "Charms" and new "Seventeen" mag. She plans to send for some more summer things. Boy, the prices – little cotton dresses $10 and up. If prices continue shooting like this, I'm afraid Daddy will have to rob a bank or something to get me clothed in a few months from now!!*

In 1942, the War Production Board limited how much cotton and other materials could be used in textiles. By 1945, there were severe shortages and prices were rising rapidly. The Office of Price Administration had put price controls on clothing in March 1945 to help prevent inflation, but they were lifted in August and costs rose again.

* * *

I don't want to disillusion you folks, but Callahan was in here the other morning making "rounds" and from what he said I got the impression that I'm not going to get a privilege as soon as I thought. He said something about waiting 6 months from the time they had surgery 'til they got "up on privileges." That would be in July. Whether he means full priv & exercise by "up on privileges" or just starting them, I don't know, but at any rate he said I'd be home going to school in the Fall. And what is 2 or 3 months when I've been here almost 3 yrs and will have many good years ahead. That's the way I figure it, but still it's hard to be patient when I feel so good in this swell spring weather. Nothing has gone wrong with my condition, you understand – I'm coming along beautifully, but I guess I just misunderstood all that rosy colored encouragement they were handing out. When they say – "You'll be going to the dining room before long" it means in about 6 months! I've found that out!! Read the April "Seventeen" from cover to cover already and there was a good article about learning to dance in it. Boy, that's one of the things Keith and I are going to do when I get home. Then if we start collecting records and get a phonograph – well, we can learn together. I'm sure looking forward to doing a lot of things and having some fun with that swell <u>big</u> brother of mine. We'll be more the same age and have more the same interests than ever before, I think.

TUESDAY [APRIL 9]

Guess who I have for a roommate? Fanchon was moved in with me yesterday and we have been having a lot of fun together. She is feeling better and will just be with me these two weeks before surgery again. Lucille is in with Sally a few doors down so all of the "gang" is at this end of the hall. Nice! Gee, practically everyone on this floor has had surgery or will have it. Fan and I get along swell – she said to thank you folks for the nice card and letter. She hasn't gotten around to write much yet.

FRIDAY [APRIL 12]

Thank you for those nice letters this week, mom. Enjoyed all the news. Thanks for the money, Daddy.

APRIL 15, 1946 [MONDAY]

Yesterday there were so many visitors and was I <u>lonesome</u> for you folks! I'm just counting the days now until you folks get here Saturday. Hope you can bring some good stuff to eat for me. I'm all out of food and have a craving for eats – things like rolls or doughnuts from the bakery – not so much for *cookies, tho. Also, could you bring me some fruit? Especially oranges. The reason I never send in to Walker for groceries is because they practically rob you. It's almost a black market, and they have such poor fruit anyway. Fanch and I are getting along so* super*!! We both like "creative" things and we even talk about opening our own shop for selling fancywork, artistic place cards, gift wrapping, and flower arranging would be our specialties. I think it would be fun but of course we're just daydreaming. Fanch doesn't cough anymore and hardly raises anything so she must be turning negative. So glad this surgery is doing the trick for her and that she has a good collapse.*

■ Fanchon had been a beautician in Mankato, so the two roommates spent a lot of time on manicures and makeup.

[GAP IN LETTERS FOR EASTER AND HER FAMILY'S VISIT]

TUESDAY [APRIL 23]
It was super to visit with you but just the same, wish Grams could have come, too. Maybe she can come in July when you can take me out for a ride around the lake, etc. Everything is going on just about the same as ever but it's awfully dead and quite a let-down from the exciting weekend.

SATURDAY MORN [APRIL 27]
Yesterday I received a letter from Helen thanking me for the elephant.

■ Marilyn had made a stuffed elephant for Mary Lynn, daughter of her cousin Helen Nelson in Iowa City. "Mary Lynn cuddles it up to her little fat face and 'coos' over it, just like she does when she loves Shelb or me," wrote Helen. She and her husband Shelby were teachers who later moved to Duluth.

* * *

The nurses tell me that Fanchon is coming along well. She had the pack removed and was sewed up so she's all through. I asked "Doc" Crow if she could room with me again in 2 weeks and he said it was okay with him.

P.S. I had my x-ray and blood test Thurs. morning and did I have fun down at the lab!!

MONDAY MORN [APRIL 29]

Beautiful morning – oh boy! If only I could go for a little after-breakfast stroll (sigh!) Did you hear Fred Allen last night at 7? His topic of discussion in Allen's Alley was about the raise in postal employees' pay. Does that affect Daddy if the bill goes through? Am sending for some cute ballerina wedgie play shoes that were advertized in the Golden Rule ad in yesterday's paper. Only $3.00 and nice for summer.

WEDNESDAY, MAY 1

It's still awfully dead here at Ching but the weather has been perfect and everyone has Spring fever including me! Last night Joanie was over to deliver mail and she told me she would be going home on May 19th. Only 19 more days! Will I ever miss her. Golly! Had some of that wonderful corn yesterday that you brought up. I gave Fan some and it was about the only thing she ate for supper. She's getting along swell and will probably be back with me on Monday. Harriet isn't feeling so good. Was over to Vera's last night for a little chat. Ardis and I talk to each other through our windows cuz we're so close. Lots of fun!

MAY 2ND, THURSDAY

Every day now I keep waiting and waiting for some good news about privileges to write you but nothing so far. Yesterday Joanie brought me a bouquet of wild plum blossoms she picked when they went for a walk in the woods. Yes, Mom, I sure would like some lilies of the valley and some lilacs, too, like you sent last year. I suppose the irises are out now, too.

MAY 4, 1946 [SATURDAY]

She [Fanch] is coming along swell and is so happy to be through with surgery. Harriet is feeling a little better and eating now and Tess is fine but she is such a complainer. They say she is the worst surgical they've ever had on this floor. She even wants a hypo when they take her stitches out. Ha! Mom, do you think I should send graduation cards to any of this year's class? I thought it would be nice to remember Arleen Johnson, Bev Bolstad, and Hildegarde Linner cuz they have been so nice to write and send cards since I've been up here. Day before yesterday I got my "Buskens" from the Golden Rule. You see, I ordered ballerina play shoes as a 1st choice and red nail head trim sandals as 2nd choice, just in case. When I got the package Thurs. guess what I got . . . the red wedgie sandals and they're just adorable! The middle strap is crossed in kind of a diagonal and it and the front one are trimmed with gold nail heads. They're made so good for only 3 dollars – have all-leather soles. Will they ever go good with my summer things.

MAY 8, 1946 [WEDNESDAY]

I just came back from my exam and I got a privilege! He gave me all the regular good news and said I wouldn't have to wear my binder any more. I'll start getting up now and in another week, he'll give me a 2nd privilege. Gosh, I'm happy now. Fanch is feeling fine and we get along swell but from now on it's going to be hard for her to stay in bed when I get up, just like it was with Joanie and me. Remember? Seems that if you wait long enough "your time" finally comes.

MAY 13, 1946 [MONDAY]

I got that letter from George Grim last week so I'm sending it to you today. I hope you can get the stuff for me, Daddy, and send it off this week. You decide what to put into the box yourself – although I wish you would put in a box or packet of air mail (or rather light weight) stationery because they don't have paper over there and I would like to hear from them. Did you read "I Like it Here" in the Tribune yesterday? In case you didn't save it, I'm sending it along too cuz it gives some suggestions and information. From what we hear over the radio, it sure must be getting terrible in

Europe. They say if food doesn't reach them in the next 6 weeks, a million people will die of starvation. I surely think this is the least we can do. I'm so interested in this, really folks, so could you tell me what you send in the box. I'd like to know. I'll write a letter to this boy, separately, and send it to you in a few days so you can mail it with the box.

■ On Sunday, May 5, *Minneapolis Tribune* columnist George Grim wrote about the Foster Parents Plan, which provided aid to children in war-torn Europe through rest camps, rehabilitation centers, and food packages. He said that if readers mailed a card or letter to him, he would send them the address of a boy or girl in France, Italy, Malta, Holland, or Belgium, and then they could send a food package directly to that child. On Wednesday, May 8, the one-year anniversary of VE Day, Grim wrote about the conditions in Europe, which in the aftermath of war was in unimaginable disarray. Grim said that some people had already forgotten about the war—"tragically fast." On Sunday, May 12, he reported that 1,834 cards and letters had arrived at his desk. He informed readers that preferred items were canned meats and fish, dried cereals and fruits, powdered eggs and milk, cocoa, tea, and dehydrated soups and bouillon. He suggested that they complete a postal declaration form to instruct that the package be delivered to the Red Cross if it couldn't be delivered to the address they had been given. Grim told readers about delays in aid through government channels because diplomatic talks in Paris would break down. He called on people in the Northwest (a popular label to describe Minnesota and the Dakotas) to show people in Europe that those delays were not "the doing of the ordinary little guy of you and me." By sending food packages, "they'll know we honestly care."

WEDNESDAY MORN [MAY 15]
Gosh, I was glad to hear from you yesterday! I couldn't figure out why you hadn't written for so long and here it was the trains! If Grandma B comes

in June, do you suppose she could come with you up here in July? I hope
Grams can make the trip then, too. Joanie got her discharge slip signed, so
she is busy packing and getting ready to go home Sunday.

■ The train strike was one of a series of postwar labor actions in
the wake of falling wages after wage and price controls expired. Almost 250,000 railroad engineers and trainmen nationwide went on
strike. In 1947, Congress responded to the strike wave by passing
the Taft-Hartley Act, restricting the powers and activities of labor
unions.

SATURDAY AFT. [MAY 18]
I suppose you've been wondering why I haven't written. Gee, I just forgot I
guess cuz I've been so busy. The train strike will be on, too, so you probably
won't receive this card for several days.

SUNDAY, MAY 19, 1946
Dear Keith,
You are confirmed by now, as this is Sunday afternoon, so congratula-
tions, honey! I've been thinking of you all morning and wishing I could
be home with you and going to church with the folks cuz this really is a
very important day in your life. It seems like such a short time ago that it
was my confirmation day and how thrilled and excited I was, too. Time
certainly moves fast – here I am – going on 19 yrs (pretty soon I won't
be able to call myself a "teenager") and my "little" brother is no longer
little. Keith, won't it be fun again when we can be together again this fall?
I know we're going to have some wonderful times together and then we
can really talk. It was a pretty big day for my former roommate, Joan,
too, because she went home for good today after being away for 2 yrs.
She was such a lovely girl and I love her just like a sister. After the show
Thursday afternoon, a bunch of the gals from CII took pictures with me
outside. We had a lot of fun and I hope they turn out good. After the show
I talked to my Indian friend, Richard Morgan, and it was nice to see him

up and around again. This week he said he'd come over to see me some time so I hope it isn't tonight while I'm gone. In this day of so much racial prejudice and discrimination, the "San" surely is a wonderful example of how all types of people can get along together. I guess when you come to think of it though, there's really no question about it . . . we just <u>have</u> to get along.

WEDNESDAY MORN [MAY 22]

Just have time for a note this morning cuz I have so many things to do. The hydrangea plant that Grandma sent me for Easter is still nice & fresh. In fact it's got to looking nicer since I've had it here in the window. One of these nights Fanch is going to teach me to play cribbage and then some of the fellows are coming down so we can play a 4-handed game. It seems pretty complicated to me now but it looks like fun. Haven't heard from Joanie as yet but she said she'd write as soon as they got settled. Boy, I could hardly say goodbye to her on Sunday cuz I had such a big lump in my throat.

SATURDAY MORN. [MAY 25]

I don't know how soon you'll get this letter but tho't I'd write anyway. These strikes sure are bunk! And do the patients up here ever miss the mail. I imagine Daddy hasn't been too busy on the mail route the last few days if he's gone at all. Gee, I'm anxious to hear from you. We've been more or less cut off from the outside world by the rail strike. What a mess! Fanch is starting fancywork again. Dr. Crow gave her permission this morning. She gets out of bed when the nurses make it up every morning, too, so she's getting stronger all the time. She feels swell and is gaining weight again. I weigh 123-125 lbs., by the way. Mr. Snyder has been sick again.

MON. MORN. [MAY 27]

I got the flowers and they were swell – lasted quite a while and did they ever perfume our room nice. Got a letter from Joanie this morning and some "pix." *She's swell and having a grand time at home. It will probably be a month and a half before I get full privileges or can take my own bath.*

[UNEXPLAINED GAP IN LETTERS]

SUNDAY, JUNE 16

Whew! Is this ever a hot day. I'm just sizzling and <u>I mean sizzling</u>. It must be about 100° right now and we just got through with supper. I have to get ready for church before long. Last night, Molly Frame died at 5:45 in the morning. I took up a collection on CII. We got over $10.00 and will send it to her husband with a card. Sure feel sorry for him – he was with her when she went.

⬛ Molly's husband, Floren, a war veteran, died a year later of heart failure at age thirty-two. He had worked at Ah-gwah-ching as a farmhand before entering military service.

JUNE 20, 1946, THURS. EVE.

Gee, I'm sorry I didn't get a letter or at least a card off to you folks this morning. I've been leading a pretty busy life this week, believe it or not. This morning I pressed a few things, got ready for the show, and then this afternoon went to the show and had my art lesson afterwards. By the way, the movie was "Rhapsody in Blue," the life of George Gershwin. Oh, I just fell in love with Robert Alda in the picture – and that music! I've gotten a lot stronger from my privileges. I don't get tired hardly at all anymore and most of my pains are gone. Those never were bad, but those needle-sticking ones were annoying when the nerves started repairing in my incisions. They're doing surgery today and are Fanch & I glad we're not among the "victims." Now we have no one real sick on our floor except Margaret Engelking and she is just hanging on and that's all. She has gotten so emaciated she looks like those pictures of people in concentration camps during the war. Harriet is next to Ardis on the other side of us now and doing okay. I guess there are just loads of patients entering now and it's almost impossible to find a vacancy in the B building.

JUNE 26TH [WEDNESDAY]

I guess something must be wrong with the trains because lately your letters & cards have been taking 2 days. Glad to hear from you. Wish I could go on a picnic like you had. Yesterday I went up to the trunk room and got down my yellow shorts. They're too small. I'll need a good dress to wear for Sunday real soon.

FRIDAY NOON [JUNE 28]

Well I got the box of things this morning and thanks loads for the nylons, panties & slip – a few more things to add to my collection. When you write to Alice, I wish you could find out about a light-weight coat. Otherwise I'd like to get one of those station wagon coats – they're rain resistant – or a topper rain coat of that shiny material. They'd be warm enough for the rest of this summer. Noticed in the paper that Donaldson's is having an End of the Month sale. Maybe Auntie Ruth could have found me a cute dress there. Anyway, I think I'll write to her and send some money for the shoes & dress. Think she kind of enjoys shopping for me, and it's easier to find things in the Cities than in St. Peter.

JUNE 29, 1946, SATURDAY EVE

Dr. Crow said I could take my own tub bath tomorrow morning and Monday noon I'll go to dinner in the dining room. Suppose I'll go to one meal for a week and then the other two the next week. Gosh, I can't believe this all is actually happening to lil' ole' me! This morning I combed Olga's hair out for her and "saw her off." She was so excited and happy to be going home for a 2-week visit. Boy, I'm so thrilled to think that the next time I come home it'll be <u>for good</u>! I'm not ever going to break down again and have to be in a San – I've made up my mind to that! Fanch and I are going to give a party on the night of the Fourth. It is to be a farewell party – sort of – for me as I'll be leaving CII soon. We're going together on the eats and thought we'd treat everyone to Cheerios. Today Fanch got another big box of food from home. We'll really be stuffing ourselves again for the next week

with bananas, apples, tomatoes, cookies, cherries, & candy. Whew! We're
the biggest pigs in Ching – no kidding, and when we have pie, ice cream or
cake for dinner, we always order "seconds" & get them. The other night we
were making sandwiches about nine-thirty when we had a Ray Milland
experience. A nice big bat flew in and boy, did we duck under the covers.
Since all the windows in the place were open, I'll bet that they heard us
scream all over the place.

■ In the 1945 movie *Lost Weekend*, Milland's alcoholic character
Don has delirium tremens and hallucinates a bat swooping in and
eating a mouse.

MONDAY MORN [JULY 1]
In a half hour or so I'll get ready for communion in the chapel. I'm going
to wear my nylons for the first time and also my dress. I have a "date" to
eat my first meal in the dining room with Mr. Snyder. Did you listen to the
Atom bomb test yesterday? We were glued to the radio all afternoon.

■ The atom bomb test on Bikini Atoll was on July 1, 1946, on the
western side of the International Date Line, but for people in the
United States, the test occurred on Sunday, June 30.

JULY 2, 1946, TUES. EVE.
Oh, it's so wonderful to eat in the dining room! Honestly it was such a thrill
to put my feet under a table again and the dining room is such a beautiful
place. You can be sure I didn't eat much the first day – I just sat and looked
around at everything and could hardly believe I actually was there and not
just dreaming. Everyone is so wonderful to me – so friendly. I sat with Mr.
Snyder the first day and today Elmer asked me to sit in a booth with him
so we did. Then Art Hegna, Helen Meindel [Meindl], and George Johnson
came and sat down with us. Sitting around those circular tables it was just
like a little family. Art mentioned several times how straight I walk. I think
my posture and walk have improved so much since I've been on the cure &
had surgery. They stress "straightness" so much after surgery to the thoro

cases. There is such a good bunch of kids on exercise and they go on wiener roasts, picnics, and fish fries together. Al Strom and a few other older men have outboard motors on their boats so they take the kids fishing with them once in a while. I can hardly wait to get over to DII now. Starting next Sunday I'll go to all my meals, I think, and then in a week I'll probably move over. I'm making my own bed now and feel so much stronger every day. Elsie Bergen may go home this weekend so I'm going to get her bed on Star Porch. It has a lovely view with windows on 3 sides.

▓ A favorite spot for patients was Buck's Landing by Leech Lake. A path led from the sanatorium to the lake, where they could sit at a picnic table and watch birds and fishermen. Later, when on exercise herself, Marilyn helped with an outdoor egg and bacon breakfast as a farewell party for Harriet Nelson.

FRIDAY [JULY 5]

We had a lovely party last night and all the girls had such a good time. It will be the last time we'll all get together before I move. Gee, I don't know

Patients having a lakeside campfire and picnic

when you should come up – I'd rather have you wait until later rather than before Keith starts detassling, because I'd like to go out to the cabin.

▓ Keith had a summer job walking cornfields for the Green Giant canning company in Le Sueur. Detasseling is a way to control the pollination of the ears of corn. In addition to producing more uniform kernels, the resulting hybrid corn also brings higher yields.

* * *

Got your cards, but I wish you'd write letters once in a while. I don't get hardly any letters these days. Are you going to send more moola? (I hope)

SUNDAY EVE, JULY 7, 1946

Tonight I'm "home" for a change so guess I'll get a start on tomorrow's letter. You know what? I'm awfully lonesome for you tonite. Wish you could come up to see me soon cuz if you wait to take me home it'll be way in Sept. or the first of Oct. You see – I want you to come while summer is still here so I can go out for a ride and see some of this lake country before I get home. Being that you and all the close relatives are so far away I'll never see any of it cuz it doesn't look like any will be coming unless you do. Maybe Wesley and Amy Kohl will invite me over to their cottage like they promised once before but so far they haven't even come up to visit yet. This morning I took another tub bath and ah! What luxury!! I poured lots of cologne in the water – very extravagant but the way I look at it – I deserve it after having bed baths for so long.

19. LOOKING TOWARD HOME

It was the most perfect day

DII, JULY 16, 1946

Here I am in my cozy lil' corner in "Sleepy Hollow." That's the old name for our ward. Although it doesn't seem very sleepy right now. Jonesy is crocheting, Bernice is reading, and "Pinky" our little redhead, is chattering away and sewing. It's rest hour so everyone is in bed. Golly, folks, I sure like it over here – I'm my own boss now and that's what I like! All the kids are so nice to me and they have made me feel like one of them already. Last night Helen Meindal [Meindl] and Ada Kray were singing some crazy old songs in the bathroom as we were getting washed & ready for bed. Then when I got back to my bed, Jonesy had beef sandwiches with catsup, radishes, & a bottle of milk waiting for us. I was just famished, too, cuz being up more gives me a huge appetite. Ah – and did I sleep soundly last night. We cover up and have all the windows wide open. There's something about the air and the sound of a motor boat out on the lake after lights-out that makes you sleep so good all wrapped up warm & snug in your blankets. I was glad to get your 2 letters yesterday, Mom & Daddy. Now I can hardly wait until August when you'll be up.

JULY 19, 1946 [FRIDAY]

I'm sitting here at my table in front of the window and it's such a beautiful day! There are big white clouds drifting by in the blue and the grove of tall pines makes a perfect setting. I've been a busy gal this morning. Right after breakfast I made my bed and took a shower – then put up my hair.

Gee, I feel so nice & clean! Yesterday after supper I was lying on top of the bed resting when one of the office girls called me out to the reception room – someone to see me. So I ran a comb through my hair and jumped into my shoes. Well, honestly, I was so shocked – standing there were Mr. & Mrs. Kutz from Stillwater. They made a special trip out here just to see me and also Palmer Anderson – Ralph's roommate on CIII. We sat and talked for an hour – all about Ralph and they were so interested in how I was coming along. I felt so very ashamed of myself for never even writing them a card after Ralph's death but I didn't have their address. Mr. Kutz is such a wonderful man and I could tell he took it very hard. They still hold it against Dr. Crow for not notifying them of Ralph's condition. They got the call ½ hour before he passed away. Richard, the baby, is a yr old now and he's a doll. I saw all the pictures of him and if he isn't just the picture of Ralph! Mrs. Kutz said he laughs just exactly like he did, too, and I'm so glad because in some way he will be able to take his older brother's place. They gave me the most gorgeous basket of fruit and candy wrapped in cellophane and tied with yards of green satin ribbon. I appreciated it so much. I suppose they did it in memory of Ralph. From what they said, Ralph was pretty fond of me and I sure thought he was pretty swell too. I guess I never realized it until I saw them yesterday. Oh, how I wish he could have lived! After the lights were out last night I cried for a while before I went to sleep. I can hardly wait until Monday. Elmer and Ernie promised to "show me around." They are good kids. Ernie is just 16 years old and he blushes something terrific. They kid him about being "sweet sixteen" and never been kissed and I always stick up for him. Yesterday he played a game of Chinese checkers with me and did he skunk me! Elmer isn't handsome or anything but he says the funniest things all the time. I had just sat down to write this when they came up from outside and Elmer handed me the biggest bouquet of wild roses you've ever seen. I've got the bouquet on my window sill and, well, can't you just smell them?

JULY 23 [TUESDAY]

Sorry I didn't get around to writing you yesterday but honestly I'm so busy I don't know what's what. In the morning I took my first 15 minutes of walking exercise and oh, it really was grand. We just go around here on the grounds because it would take longer than 15 minutes to get down the road and back. Tomorrow George Johnson is going to take me to the farm and show me the pet kittens. Last Saturday nite we had the most fun! All of the boys from DIII came downstairs and we had a Coke party. We sat on chairs arranged in a circle and played all kinds of parlor games. Gosh, what a riot! We laughed and whooped it up until the nite supervisor broke it up at 9:15. Honestly, I haven't had so much fun since those Luther League parties. Yesterday Harriet moved in with me and she's a swell pal. Thanks for the music – I just love that Gershwin tune and have been practicing it on the piano in the chapel. Beverly Pantzke, a new gal from BIII just moved down here and she has lots of popular pieces that she plays, too. This morning the two of us walked down to the lab for gastric lavage (stomach wash culture) – Wow! What an experience to swallow and gag on that rubber hose! Mur-der! I also sent out another sputum culture this morning so if and when they come back negative it will be about the same time I finish exercise. Then Dr. Cal said he'd "talk business" with me about going back to St. Peter.

▧ A gastric lavage involved having a tube inserted through the mouth or nose to go down the esophagus into the stomach. A small amount of stomach liquid was collected and tested for tuberculosis bacteria. The contents had to be negative for a patient to be discharged.

* * *

Guess what! I got the biggest surprise of my life on Saturday! You know some time ago I wrote a fan letter & sent the "Moc" with the poem to Van Johnson. Well, I got a beautiful autographed photo of him and also a nice letter wishing me an early recovery. The photo was signed, "To Marilyn Barnes, Kindest regards, Van Johnson". I sure wish you could have heard the gals scream when I got it.

Van Johnson autographed his publicity photo for Marilyn

Van Johnson's letter

Dear Marilyn Barnes. Thank you for your nice letter. I was particularly interested to read your magazine, especially page nine. I'm glad to know you enjoy my work in pictures and think it was really swell of you to write and tell me so. I'm sending you a picture which I hope that you will accept with my best wishes for your early recovery.

JULY 27, 1946 [SATURDAY]

Gee, this sure has been a cool week but the sun has shone every day so I've been able to go outside. And does this air and exercise ever make me sleep good! I eat like a horse – honest! I get chocolate milk every day from the dining room – for our evening lunch, and we can buy Cokes and "Squirt" from the store so we have plenty to drink. This afternoon I'm going over to visit on CII – haven't seen Fanchon & Olga for so long that I'm very ashamed, but gosh, it's real hard to ask for passes all the time. Be sure and let me know when you are coming up – I sure hope you can make it on the 10th. Cabins aren't so very hard to get and I'm sure you'll be able to stay at Paradise Point again. Food is terribly hard to get around here so I suppose you'll have to bring most of your own. Lucy Niesen is ready to be discharged now but she is an orphan so she is going to start working here as a nurses' aide.

JULY 31, 1946 [WEDNESDAY]

Received your card this morning, Mom, and I'm glad to hear you are coming the 9th Then probably we can go to Brainerd on Saturday, huh? Last night Amy Kohl with Doug and Dorothy drove over to invite me out to their lake cottage. Well, I got the permission this morning and Doug stopped by at 11 to find out so he's driving up to get me tomorrow (Thurs.) morning at 10:30 to take me out. And I imagine I'll stay until after supper.

▓ Wesley and Amy Kohl, friends of Marilyn's uncle Gerold, had a summer home on Ten Mile Lake near Hackensack. Marilyn knew Wes because he had been the organist for silent films at the old movie theater in St. Peter.

* * *

Now about our party for George. Well, it surely was a huge success last night. I led the games and everyone – especially some of the old men like Mr. Snyder, etc., said they hadn't had so much fun in years. George appreciated it so much and told us girls how much fun he had. I sure got a big lump in my throat when he left on the bus this morning although I was happy he could leave because he's been here 4 yrs and practically grown up at Ching. When he got on the bus he didn't even look back cuz he was almost on the verge of breaking down – poor kid. Yesterday the re-habilitation man was here and talked with all of us new patients on DII. He helps the tubercular get on their feet after being discharged – helping them to get jobs – paying part of their way to schools, etc. He certainly is a nice fellow and I told him about my wanting to study art. He had

Miss Lyford give me some aptitude, interest, and personality tests this morning and oh, they were fun! He'll come again in 2 weeks so then I'll find out the results.

▩ Because sanatorium patients were considered to be disabled, they were eligible for funding for education or training for employment. The representative informed Marilyn that, based on the tests, she was suited for beauty college or secretarial work. When she arrived home, a different representative called on her. She told him she wanted to go to college, and that she would like to go to Gustavus Adolphus in St. Peter so that she could stay at home and be taken care of. He agreed to the plan, and her first semester cost, about $100, was paid for.

AUGUST 2, 1946 [FRIDAY]

First of all, I had the most wonderful holiday at Ten-Mile-Lake! Oh, I haven't had such a wonderful time since I've been up here. Doug came and got me at 10:30 a.m. and first we went to Hackensack to get ice cream. Then we drove out along the lake and he pointed out the different homes and cottages. When we got to "the Hermitage," we tip-toed in the back door as Amy and the two kids hadn't told Wes I was coming. He was standing with his back to me and you should have seen the look on his face when he saw me. Honestly, the poor man couldn't speak – as he was just going to ask Amy about going up to the San to see "Marilyn" one of these days. Wes sure is a good fellow – they all are, for that matter, and I felt so at home with them. We had a wonderful dinner. We sat down on the "Lookout" a kind of deck for their lawn chairs, built right over the lake and talked until it was one and then everyone took a rest hour until 2. I took a short cat nap in the guest house, which they call "The Hut." It's made of real logs and decorated in knotty pine. Then at 3, Doug took Dorothy and me out for a speed boat ride. Was that fun! We went skimming around the lake at 30 or more miles per hour and it was the most perfect day. We went around the whole lake and when I got back my hair was a wreck but who was I to care. I was having so darned much fun. We had kind of a picnic supper on the porch overlooking the lake and for dessert, apple pie a-la-mode. After supper the 3 of us kids went for another speed boat ride just as the sun was setting and we chased crazy loons all over the lake. We started back to the San shortly before eight.

▧ Imagine all that excitement after being in the sanatorium for almost three years. It was a day that Marilyn never forgot, a gift from friends who knew she was negative and didn't worry about being "contaminated." A few days after her adventure, her parents arrived to stay at a resort and visit with her. They went out for drives in the area and made plans for Marilyn's homecoming, which occurred on September 7.

EPILOGUE

MARILYN LATER SAID, "I NEVER, EVER THOUGHT I WAS GOING TO die. I knew I was going to get well. Even when I was so sick, I was still fighting to stay alive. I had so many people praying for me. I had Catholic neighbors named O'Brien who went and made novenas for me. Everyone from our church, they were so supportive. And all my relatives, too."

Marilyn was still a junior when she returned to high school in St. Peter, attending only half days at first so she could get enough rest. Mentally and emotionally, she felt ancient compared to her classmates. She had been exposed to so many life situations, so much sadness and loss. When some girls were afraid to have a Mantoux test because of the needle, Marilyn said, "Needles. You don't know what needles are." When Marilyn graduated with honors, she received an award for courage from the local American Legion post. After graduation, she looked for a summer job, applying at the local greenhouse. Marilyn heard later that she didn't get the position because the owner's wife was afraid of TB. It didn't make any difference that Marilyn had been released with papers attesting that she was healed.

When Marilyn was a sophomore at Gustavus Adolphus College, she wanted to apply to work at a national park with some of her friends, but when she mentioned the idea to Dr. Callahan during an annual checkup, he vetoed it. He suggested instead that she work as a nurse's aide at Ah-gwah-ching, where they would be able to monitor her health. She was assigned to the Indian Building, where, in a reversal of her own experience, she gave bed baths to Native American

men. "That was a really crazy experience," she said. "I could never figure out what they laughed about. They had such a strange sense of
humor. I would come in and tell a joke. Just a straight face from the
Indian men. Then they would say something, and they would laugh,
and I had no idea what they were laughing about."

She resumed her correspondence with her family, in both letters
and postcards. On July 8, 1949, she wrote, "If anyone ever feels like
sending me some fresh cookies or rolls or coffee cake, don't hesitate.
Ha! General hint. See—I still haven't forgotten how to beg!!"

Marilyn met her "good healthy fella" at Gustavus Adolphus College. She married William Robertz in 1953. Marilyn taught art classes
at White Bear Lake High School and in Illinois and Michigan while
Bill attended graduate school. They returned to St. Peter, where they
raised their children, Paul and Ruth. Bill taught speech at Gustavus
Adolphus for thirty-eight years. In 1999, Marilyn was interviewed
for and appeared in the PBS documentary *Tuberculosis: The People's
Plague*, produced by Florentine Films.

Marilyn listened to the parting advice from staff at Ah-gwah-ching:
"Live a life of routine. Get plenty of rest and eat well. Remember all of
the things you learned at the sanatorium about good health." Marilyn
celebrated her ninetieth birthday on October 3, 2017.

ACKNOWLEDGMENTS

THIS BOOK OWES ITS EXISTENCE TO THE LEGACY RESEARCH FEL-lowship I received from the Minnesota Historical Society in 2015. Without it, I would not have plumbed the depths of archival material about Ah-gwah-ching State Sanatorium to discover the Marilyn Barnes Robertz collection of letters. On the other hand, without the assistance of Marilyn herself, it might have been impossible to develop a cohesive story. Marilyn graciously answered many questions about her three-year experience and the letters' contents. I am pleased that we have become friends.

For recommending me as a Legacy Research Fellow, I am grateful to Jim Northrup, who was at Ah-gwah-ching as a child in 1946, and to Freya Manfred, whose parents met at Glen Lake Sanatorium.

A thank-you goes to Shannon Pennefeather at the Minnesota Historical Society Press for encouraging me to publish the letters. I appreciate her thoughtful advice and comments throughout an editing and annotating process that was new to me. Thank you to Laura Drew, whose cover design visually places Marilyn's story in its era.

I thank the reference assistants and copy center staff at the Gale Family Library in the Minnesota History Center. They are essential partners in any state history project. Like Scouts, they are helpful, friendly, courteous, kind, and cheerful.

I am grateful for the support of the monthly researchers' group at the Minnesota Historical Society. I can't say it any better than group member Cheri Register: "There is no encouragement like the empathy of fellow obsessives."

There were many teachers, instructors, and mentors in my life. Two special ones were Bertha Thorson Rummel, who taught me how to read, and Alida Mathison Brecke, who didn't laugh at my fifth-grade efforts at writing. Others who encouraged me to write or helped me become a better writer were Areta Wold, Clara Lund, Allison McGhee, Susan Perry, and Mary Williams.

Special thanks go to my husband, Verdell, and my daughters Jennie, Jill, and Josie and their families for their patience and support. Writing two books about historical tuberculosis has many times been an inconvenient intrusion into our "real life." I love you all.

NOTES

1. J. Arthur Myers, *Invited and Conquered: Historical Sketch of Tuberculosis in Minnesota* (Minnesota Public Health Association, 1949), 432.
2. G. R. Duncan, E. P. K. Fenger, and A. B. Greene, "The Treatment of Pulmonary Tuberculosis by Hyperpyrexia: A Preliminary Report," *American Review of Tuberculosis* (1933): 28, 752.
3. J. D. Boice Jr., D. Preston, F. G. Davis, and R. R. Monson, "Frequent Chest X-Ray Fluoroscopy and Breast Cancer Incidence Among Tuberculosis Patients in Massachusetts," *Journal of Radiation Research* 125, no. 2 (February 1991): 214–22.
4. John Weinzirl, "The Action of Sunlight upon Bacteria with Special Reference to B. Tuberculosis," *Journal of Infectious Diseases* 4, supplement 3 (May 1907): 128–53.
5. Norman Rusten's obituary at https://www.findagrave.com/memorial /41770833/norman-rusten.
6. *Joyce Lamont's Favorite Minnesota Recipes & Radio Memories* (Minneapolis, MN: Voyager Press, 2008).
7. "Pick-Ups," *St. Peter Herald*, 1945.

INDEX

For details about Marilyn, see entries for topics like mail, privileges, surgery, etc.; and for individuals like family members, fellow patients, and medical staff.

The Girl in Building C was designed and set in type by Judy Gilats in Saint Paul, Minnesota. The display face is Futura and the text face is Arno Pro.